TAK
AND

THE HISTORY OF
TAKESHIMA AND JAPAN

HISTORICAL ACCOUNTS AND STORIES FROM THE SAN'IN REGION

SUGIHARA TAKASHI

Japan Publishing Industry Foundation for Culture

PUBLISHER'S NOTE

This book follows the Hepburn system of romanization, with long vowels indicated by macrons. The tradition of placing the family name first has been followed for Japanese and Korean names. With the reader in mind, the content and format of the original Japanese edition has been revised and adjusted for this English edition.

The History of Takeshima and Japan: Historical Accounts and Stories from the San'in Region
Sugihara Takashi. Translated by the Japan Institute of International Affairs (JIIA).

Published by
Japan Publishing Industry Foundation for Culture (JPIC)
2-2-30 Kanda-Jinbocho, Chiyoda-ku, Tokyo 101-0051, Japan

First English edition: February 2022

© 2010 Sugihara Takashi
English translation © The Japan Institute of International Affairs (JIIA)
All rights reserved

Originally self-published in Japanese under the title *San'in chihō no rekishi ga kataru "Takeshima mondai"* in 2010.
English publishing rights arranged with the author.

This publication is the result of a collaborative effort between the Japan Institute of International Affairs (JIIA) and Japan Publishing Industry Foundation for Culture (JPIC).

Jacket and cover design by Jennifer Piatkowski

Printed in Japan
ISBN 978-4-86658-232-0
https://www.jpic.or.jp/

Table of Contents

Contemporary maps of Takeshima in relation to Japan and the Republic of Korea

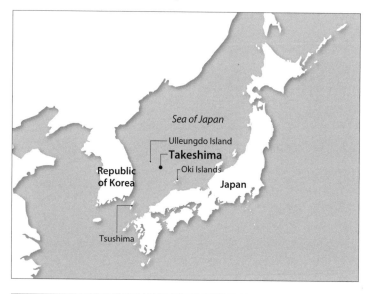

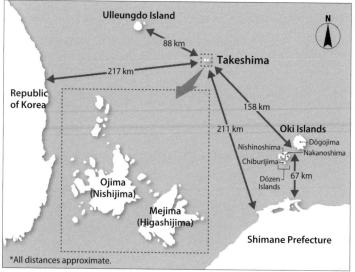

Introduction

In September 2007, I received the honor of being asked to start a series of columns for the Shimane-ken Web Takeshima Mondai Kenkyūsho (Shimane Prefectural Government's Web Takeshima Issue Research Institute). Titled the "Sugihara Tsūshin" (Sugihara News), the columns introduced my latest research on the issue. The series ended upon the completion of the thirtieth and final installment.

It all started in June 2005 when I was appointed a member of Shimane Prefecture's Takeshima Mondai Kenkyūkai (Takeshima Issue Research Group) and was asked to examine an enormous volume of documents, illustrations, and maps together with other group members. During this work, I came to the realization that the Takeshima Dispute is not simply a territorial issue about whether the islands belong to either Japan or Korea. Rather, it is a historical issue that arose from the accumulation of layer upon layer of local history, primarily in the San'in region (Shimane, Tottori, and Yamaguchi Prefectures). I also felt the need to support Japan's younger generation, in particular junior and senior high school students, by teaching them basic knowledge on the Takeshima Dispute and fostering their capacity to think constructively, since they will likely be the ones to interact with South Korean youth and go on to help resolve the problem.

In August 2008, I had finished presenting major historical issues involving Takeshima in ten installments of my column when the *Handbook* on junior high school geography announced by the Ministry of Education, Culture, Sports, Science and Technology (MEXT) pointed out the need to teach the Takeshima Dispute within Japan. In early 2009, research staff at the Web Takeshima Issue Research Institute and elementary and junior high school teachers in Shimane prepared supplementary teaching materials and early in the academic year these materials were distributed to all schools in the prefecture. In July 2009, a first-year junior high school social studies class was opened to the public at a school in Matsue City and the materials were used in the class. I was there as an observer. Forty students, who had not learned about the Takeshima Dispute in elementary school, gathered in small groups and discussed answers to questions raised in the latter part of the class. This was a deeply emotional sight for me to witness.

In December 2009, MEXT also announced the *Handbook* for senior high school geography and history classes. The *Handbook* states, "It is necessary to deepen understanding of territorial issues by accurately discussing them on the basis of the understanding that Japan's positions are legitimate, building upon what is taught in junior high school." Contrary to our expectations, the word, "Takeshima," was not explicitly used. However, I am certain that senior high school students will independently deepen their understanding of the Takeshima issue, based on what they learn in junior high school. It is my hope that the people of Japan, both young and old alike, will use the Japanese version of this book to deepen their understanding of the Takeshima Dispute and the local history of the San'in region, and that non-Japanese, both here in Japan and abroad, will reference this English edition to become more familiar with the history of the issue and Japan's stance.

1

One of Kim In-woo's Ships Drifts Ashore in Hamada

The Republic of Korea, or South Korea, has in recent years been naming parts of the seabed around Takeshima. What these places have in common is that they contain the names of historical figures related to the Takeshima Dispute. For instance, one of the seamounts was named after Kim In-woo.

Since the early 1400s, the Joseon dynasty (1392–1910) on the Korean Peninsula appointed officials in Samcheok, who were well acquainted with the area around Ulleungdo Island (鬱陵島), as chiefs tasked with arresting and bringing back those who fled to the island to avoid paying taxes, forced military service, and so on. Kim In-woo was one such chief.

Kim first arrested three people on Usando Island (干山島) in 1417 (see fig. 4 on p. 166). This Usando seems to have actually been Ulleungdo Island, but Korean researchers contend that it was Dokdo (独島), which is currently called Takeshima (竹島) in Japanese. Kim also brought back giant bamboo, water buffalo skins, and ramie. He would go out to the island many times after this for the purpose of arresting people and bringing them back to the Korean mainland.

In 1425, Kim In-woo headed to Ulleungdo with two boats and one boat unfortunately capsized. After reaching the island, Kim arrested 20 people, brought them back, and reported to King Sejong of Joseon. The king ordered that a memorial service be held for the 46 people who had been aboard the lost boat as it was deemed likely that they had all perished.

Yet something wholly unexpected took place in the twelfth month of the same year. Ten people who had been on the capsized boat suddenly appeared. Standing before the astonished Kim In-woo and other officials was a man named Jang Eulbu. He related what happened to him and the others.

He began with their boat capsizing after being struck by strong winds. Ten of the 46 men aboard were able to hold onto the boat as it drifted to a beach called Nagahama in Iwami Province, located in present-day western Shimane Prefecture. From there, the group could not walk due to fatigue, so they crawled some distance and happened upon a spring. After drinking their fill, they all passed out on the spot from exhaustion. After some time, a fisherman found them and brought them to a nearby temple where they received food. Later, they met the local lord Suntorō (the Sufu lord) who assessed their origin based on their attire. Suntorō sympathized with the group of castaway Koreans and took them under his care, assuring them that he would send them back home. A boat was prepared for them within 30 days and a farewell party was held. The group was escorted to the island of Tsushima where they met with a man named Saemontarō, a person of influence. After making some arrangements, Saemontarō was able to have the men sent back safely to Korea from Tsushima.

Upon hearing this, the Korean king was deeply moved

and immediately dispatched a man called Yi Ye to the Sufu lord Suntorō and Saemontarō. He delivered gifts of gratitude as well as a promise that they would be granted trading rights and other privileges if they come to Korea.

Suntorō was a man of importance who had a castle in what is now Sufu-chō, Hamada City. He belonged to a branch of the Masuda house through an illegitimate son. At this time, the family head was a man named Sufu Kanenaka. Kanenaka availed himself of the Korean king's offer and dispatched trading ships to Korea on six occasions. His son Kanesada and grandson Kazukane likewise sent many ships, and the Sufu clan prospered thanks to the profits from trade with Korea. The Hachimangū Shrine in Hinashi-chō has a lion dog mask that is said to have been brought back from Korea around that time.

Meanwhile, Sōda Saemontarō was the leader of a naval force on Tsushima. The lords of Tsushima were acting gov-

The lion dog mask that the Sufu clan brought back from Korea (property of Hinashi Hachimangū Shrine, Hinashi-chō, Hamada City)

ernors (*shugodai*) belonging to the Sō clan, but the Sōda clan briefly came to be more influential than the Sō thanks to profit from trade with Korea. The Sōda family is an old house that still exists today and possesses documents related to their trade with Korea during the Middle Ages. The Korean castaways who had set out with Kim In-woo to Ulleungdo drifted to Nagahama in Hamada and came to have a major, long-lasting impact on the Sufu and Sōda clans.

Moreover, until the early Meiji period (1868–1912), Korea adopted an "empty island" policy to keep Koreans from going to Ulleungdo. In that time, Japanese went to the apparently uninhabited island during the Edo period (1603–1867) to harvest the island's abundant resources in the form of timber, bamboo, abalone, and sea lions. Around 1640, present-day Takeshima was discovered by the Japanese traveling to Ulleungdo and subsequently used as a stopover, as well as a place to harvest abalone and hunt sea lions.

Pioneers to Ulleungdo (Takeshima):
Matazai and Ōya Jinkichi

Present-day Takeshima lies 158 km northwest of Oki, and Ulleungdo lies another 88 km further west.* As previously discussed, Korea adopted an "empty island" policy toward Ulleungdo by prohibiting any Koreans from living there. The Japanese noticed that the island had abundant resources and made their way there. The first person to go to Ulleungdo, whose name we know, was Matazai (presumably Matazaemon or Matazō) and others from Mihonoseki (present-day Mihonoseki-chō, Matsue City, Shimane Prefecture). Next was the merchant Ōya Jinkichi from Yonago (present-day Yonago City, Tottori Prefecture).

If we first take a look at Matazai, we find two references from the Tsushima Domain recorded in *Takeshima kōshō* (Takeshima Investigation) by Kitazawa Masanari, who compiled historical records at the Ministry of Foreign Affairs. The first is "In the second year of Genna [1616], seven people from Mihonoseki, Izumo Province, went to Takeshima to fish, were blown off course by the wind, drifted to Korea, were given a letter from the third minister of the Board of Rites [director of foreign affairs] to the Sō, and were escorted home." (The Takeshima mentioned here was the then Japanese name for

Ulleungdo at the time.) The second states, "On a total of three occasions has a letter from the third minister of the Board of Rites been given to our province and have castaways been repatriated. On one of these, 78 years ago, the Japanese man Matazai and others, residents of Mihonoseki, had gone to fish near Ulleungdo."

When I made a stop at the Kyushu National Museum in Dazaifu, Fukuoka Prefecture, on the way back from a survey of Ulleungdo in 2016, I found out about the existence of a letter there written by the Korean third minister of the Board of Rites, Yi Myeongnam (李命男), to the Tsushima lord Sō Yoshinari. The letter stated that they would send them Matazai's group and requested that they be returned to their hometown. It is dated the seventh month of Wanli 46, so we know that they were repatriated in 1618, the fourth

Letter from Yi Myeongnam to Sō Yoshinari
(property of Kyushu National Museum)

year of Genna (1615–1624) in Japan. Likewise, in a record of the Korean court, "Daily Records of Prince Gwanghaegun," in the *Veritable Records of the Joseon Dynasty*, we find an account of Matazai drifting ashore in Korea. Matazai is also mentioned to illustrate how Japanese castaways were treated with hospitality in the later *Annals of King Sukjong* and the book *Chungwanji*, a collection of case studies related to the Board of Rites. I have not been able to find the name Matazai in Mihonoseki's local documents, but it is noteworthy that people from Mihonoseki were fishing around Ulleungdo, which is further away from Japan than present-day Takeshima, during the early Edo period.

In 1617, the third year of Genna, it was the Yonago cargo merchant Ōya Jinkichi whose ship went off course as he was on his way home with cargo from Echigo (present-day Niigata Prefecture) and drifted to Ulleungdo. In the Edo period, goods were usually transported by ship. Although much later, a ship belonging to Takadaya Kahē, a so-called *kitamaebune* (北前船) from Matsumae in Hokkaido, made round trips between Hokkaido and Iwami/Nagato, passing in between Ulleungdo and Takeshima. This is recorded in the *Iwami gaiki* (Iwami External Record) which was written in the Hamada Domain (present-day Shimane Prefecture). Similarly, we know from the cargo ship records (*kaisen hikae*) of big ports like Izumosaki in Echigo that there were cargo vessels going from San'in to Echigo and Hokkaido.

It was in this context that Ōya Jinkichi's ship drifted to Ulleungdo. In *Ōya-ke komonjo* (Ōya Family Documents), we find the following: "Jinkichi went all over the island, carefully thinking about how to cross over. Korea was 40–50 *ri*

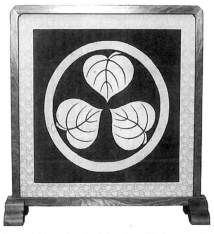

Framed ship ensign depicting the wild ginger crest used by the Ōya family of Yonago which was granted to them by the Edo *bakufu* (property of Yonago Municipal Historical Museum, Shimane Prefecture)

away and there were no houses, but there were natural resources. He thought about the situation and the possibilities of crossing the sea for some days, and then set sail for Minatoyama [present-day Yonago City]." That is, Jinkichi went around the whole island, saw that it had abundant resources, and decided to start going there regularly. Once back in Yonago, Jinkichi went with his friend Murakawa Ichibē to apply for permission to travel to the island from the *bakufu*, the samurai government of Japan during the Edo period. Permission, needed to travel far from the coast, was granted, and thus started more than 70 years of travel to Ulleungdo. During this period, they also found out about the existence of present-day Takeshima, and it came to be used as a stopover. Jinkichi himself went to Ulleungdo on several occasions and appears to have died of disease there. The ship's crew consisted mainly of townspeople from Yonago and there were always two or three men from Izumo there as well, while the ship always departed from Kumozu, Mihonoseki's outer port. It is likely that there were fishermen in Mihonoseki who, like Matazai, had gone to Ulleungdo before Jinkichi and were well acquainted with the sea route there, so it is my guess that two or three of them assisted as guides aboard the ship.

*The current distances between Takeshima and Oki and Takeshima and Ulleungdo were updated using satellite measurements.

3

Ulleungdo and Takeshima

The *Oki kokishū* (Collection of Old Writings from Oki), written by Ōnishi Noriyasu in the Edo period, states, "It is said that the fishermen of Oki can see Matsushima [present-day Takeshima] from Mount Daimanjiyama [a mountain 607 m above sea level in Okinoshima-chō] on a clear fall day when the north wind is strong." That is, the fishermen, who were used to seeing the sea, were able to look down on Takeshima 158 km away. Moreover, when I visited Ulleungdo in 2006, there was an observation deck 300 m above sea level with telescopes that let you see Takeshima 88 km away.

As mentioned previously, in an attempt to prevent Ulleungdo from becoming a haven for those evading financial and military obligation, the Joseon kingdom adopted an "empty island" policy lasting from the Muromachi period (1338–1573) to the early Meiji period. As a result, many Japanese arrived to make use of the island's abundant resources. Bamboo is a well-known product of Ulleungdo, identified as *Pseudosasa viridula* (篁竹) in Korean records, but I suspect it is *Phyllostachys edulis* (孟宗竹) from the thickness of the bamboo and the fact that the Japanese said the same kind could be found in Japan. Members of the Ōya and Murakawa families went to the island every year after receiving permission from the Edo *bakufu* and received orders for Ulleungdo bamboo from men of influence in various places to be used in ikebana, the art of flower arrangement. Eventually, present-day Ulleungdo came to be called Takeshima (lit. bamboo island, 竹島) in Japan.

In turn, present-day Takeshima was once called Matsushima (lit. pine island, 松島). It is unclear how it got that name, but one theory is that it was because small pines grew on its rocky outcroppings. Another is that it was because of the poetic association between pine, bamboo, and plum. In the Meiji period Matsushima eventually became known as Takeshima, bringing us to the present day.

The best harbor on Ulleungdo, or Takeshima as it was known in the Edo period, was called Hamadaura. Known as Dodong today, it is flanked by rocky outcroppings, protecting

"Illustration of Takeshima, Matsushima, and Oki" (*Ōya-ke yuisho jikki*, in the possession of Yonago Municipal Historical Museum)

ships from wind and waves. In his work *Takeshima zasshi* (Takeshima Magazine), the scholar Matsuura Takeshirō writes that the reason for the name Hamadaura was that "it is frequently visited by people from around Hamada in Iwami." It is true that the *Tsūkō ichiran* (Survey of Intercourse), a compilation of texts on diplomacy in the Edo period, says that commoners from Nagato (an area facing the Sea of Japan in Yamaguchi Prefecture), adjacent to Hamada, prospered by selling bamboo brought back from Ulleungdo. Moreover, when the *bakufu* later prohibited travel to Ulleungdo, a man from Hamada named Hachiemon was caught and executed for smuggling from the island. At the same time, Nagoya University professor Ikeuchi Satoshi has argued that the name Hamadaura might come from it being "a port that leads to Ulleungdo from Hamada in Iwami." Those going from Fukuura in Oki to Ulleungdo would normally head for Oki on their way back, but since they relied on the wind, they were sometimes blown off course and ended up in Hamada.

I will now turn my attention to Takeshima, which was known as Matsushima in the Edo period. In the records of the Ōya merchant family from Yonago, it is written, "Sometime after we started traveling to Ulleungdo, we discovered this island and received permission from the *bakufu* to go there as well, so we used it as a stopover and hunted sea lions there." Takeshima as seen from Ulleungdo is in the very southeast, so if one were to head directly for Ulleungdo from Oki, it is not easily spotted, which a modern-day account also attests to. The person who attested to this lived in Nishino-shima-chō, Oki District, and said that they did not see

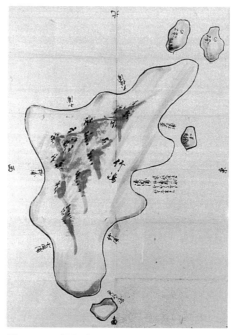

"Illustration of Takeshima" (present-day Ulleungdo)
(photo of the illustration owned by the Murakawa family,
in the possession of Yonago Municipal Historical Museum)

Takeshima once on four round-trip journeys. Moreover, in November 1951, two months prior to South Korea's unilateral establishment of the Syngman Rhee Line, Yoshioka Hiroshi and other teachers from Sakai High School (Sakaiminato City, Tottori Prefecture) were headed for Takeshima but first spotted Ulleungdo and had to hastily adjust the boat's course.

One thing that stands out about Matsushima (present-day Takeshima) in the Edo period is the enthusiasm for hunting sea lions displayed there by the Murakawa merchant family from Yonago. This is first mentioned in a letter written by the merchant Ishii Sōetsu from present-day Tottori City around 1640.

In 2006, a photograph of an Edo-period illustration said to be held by the Murakawa family was discovered (see p. 30). It is a splendid illustration that compares favorably with a modern map of Takeshima and could not have been drawn by anyone who did not actually go there frequently. I would very much like to view the original, but there is no one from the Murakawa family line in Yonago and I was not able to find any clues despite my best efforts.

Sea lions were hunted by catching them with nets and then killed or immobilized with sticks or guns. They were hunted mainly for the oil in their blubber, which was extracted by boiling them in pots. I have seen references that say one sea lion could yield several *to* of oil (1 *to* is 10 *shō* or approx. 18 liters), which was brought back in tubs. In 1905, when Takeshima became part of Goka Village of Oki District, Oki residents were granted permission by Shimane Prefecture to form companies to hunt sea lions on Takeshima. The number of sea lions caught increased from about 1,300 in 1906, to 2,000 in 1907, and 1,800 in 1908. It is possible that there were more sea lions on Takeshima in the Edo period when the Murakawa family hunted there.

4

The Ōya and
Murakawa Families

Having been granted permission from the *bakufu* to cross over to Ulleungdo, which was called Takeshima at the time, Yonago townspeople from the Ōya and Murakawa families took turns making annual trips via Oki for more than 70 years.

The Ōya family originates from Ōyadani in Tajima Province (present-day northern Hyōgo Prefecture). In 1617, a man called Ōya Jinkichi (he later changed the characters for his family name from 大屋 to 大谷) drifted to Ulleungdo and took note of its abundant resources. He died at a young age due to disease during one of his visits to the island after having started a business of collecting island resources and shipping them to mainland Japan.

Jinkichi's business was then inherited by his nephew Ōya Katsumune. He called himself Kyūemon and so every new Ōya family head would take on the name Kyūemon. Kyūemon Katsumune secured the foundation for travel to Ulleungdo and died at the age of ninety-seven in 1662. Next to inherit the business was Kyūemon Katsuzane.

To show appreciation for having been granted permission by the *bakufu* to travel to the island, members of the Ōya and Murakawa families frequently traveled to Edo to present gifts to the shogun or *bakufu* lords. One record lists a gift of 500 dried abalones to the shogun and to the members of the council of elders (*rōjū*), and a gift of 300 to the chamberlain (*sobayōnin*), the junior elders (*wakadoshiyori*), and the commissioner of shrines and temples (*jisha bugyō*). They had audiences with the shogun called *omemie* (御目見得) where they presented the gifts directly to the shogun and were asked about Ulleungdo.

Katsuzane had an *omemie* with the fourth Tokugawa shogun, Ietsuna, in 1659 and 1671. Katsuzane died in 1679 and was succeeded by Kyūemon Katsunobu. During his time, a *bakufu* inspector came to the San'in region in 1681. There is a record of Katsunobu offering his house in Nadachō, Yonago, as accommodation and answering questions about Ulleungdo, which has drawn the attention of researchers. Katsunobu died in 1692 and Kyūemon Katsufusa, aged seven, became the new family head.

This was also the year when people who had gone to Ulleungdo on a ship owned by the Murakawa family encountered a group of Koreans, which had never happened before. The Koreans rebuked them, telling them that the island was theirs and to never come there again. When a ship belonging to the Ōya family went to Ulleungdo the next year, they were greeted by a larger group of Koreans, who were using Japanese huts and small boats without permission. They returned to Yonago, taking with them two men called An Yong-bok and Pak Eo-dun. We know that they departed Ulleungdo, arrived in Fukuura in Oki after a two-day journey, made a stop at Nagahama in Izumo via Dōzen, the group of three islands that are part of the Oki Islands, and then arrived home in Yonago. The two Koreans stayed with the Ōya family in Yonago for some time, and the family treated them as guests. A little over a month later, they were taken by land to the castle town of Tottori in the domain of the same name. A few days later, they headed to Nagasaki together with two escort retainers, a doctor, a chef, and others. They arrived in Nagasaki over three weeks later. From there, they returned home via Tsushima, and we can find a record of what An Yong-bok said in Tsushima Domain in *Takeshima kiji* (Records of Takeshima) and what happened after their return to Korea in the *Annals of King Sukjong*.

The *bakufu* had Tsushima Domain negotiate the status of Ulleungdo with Korea over the following three years, but these talks did not lead anywhere, partially because of Tsushima's obstinate stance. Thus, the *bakufu* decided to prohibit Japanese travel to Ulleungdo in 1696. As for the Ōya family's reaction to the news, it is written in the *Ōya-ke yuisho jikki* (True Record of the Ōya Family History) that "the king of Korea was enraged that we had arrested An Yong-bok and Pak Eo-dun, so the *bakufu* produced documentary evidence that Takeshima [Ulleungdo] belongs to Japan, had the king of Korea acknowledge this, and then let the Koreans have the island for a period of time."

Having lost his livelihood, which relied on traveling to and from Ulleungdo, Kyūemon Masafusa decided to move to Izumo and applied for the domain's permission to do so. It is likely that he turned to his older sister who had married into the Satō family in Kamo Village, Ōhara District (present-day Kamo-chō, Unnan City, Shimane Prefecture). I examined the *Kamochō-shi* (Kamo Town Gazette) and found that there were several townspeople whom the domain allowed to have the family name of Satō, but it is currently unclear which Satō it was. In response, the Tottori Domain decided against allowing the pedigreed Ōya family to move to another domain, and instead had them become fish and fowl wholesalers in Yonago. The Ōya family devoted themselves to this wholesale business, and by the time of family head Kyūemon Katsuoki in the 1800s, they were wealthy enough to contribute funds to Tottori Domain on an annual basis.

Let us now turn to the Murakawa family. The lineage started with the warrior Yamada Jirōsaemon Masanari, who served Hisamatsu Kai no Kami in Settsu (present-day Osaka), but he died committing seppuku, after which his son Masakazu followed his mother to Yonago, as she was the daughter of Murakawa Rokurōzaemon of Yonago. He then took his mother's maiden name of Murakawa.

Masakazu and his successor Masasato both went by the name Jinbē, but the name Ichibē was subsequently used by later heads, starting with Masasato's successor Masazumi. This Ichibē Masazumi of the Murakawa family was a good friend of Ōya Jinkichi. After Jinkichi drifted to Ulleungdo, it was Ichibē who applied to the *bakufu* for permission to travel to the island and made that travel a reality. He continued to be passionate about this business even after Jinkichi's death, cultivated a close relationship with the *bakufu*, and enjoyed the honor of having an *omemie* at Edo Castle on three occasions in 1626, 1638, and 1645. We know from the letters of the Tottori merchant Ishii Sōetsu and the *Illustration of Matsushima*, which is said to be held by the Murakawa family (the whereabouts of the original is currently unknown,

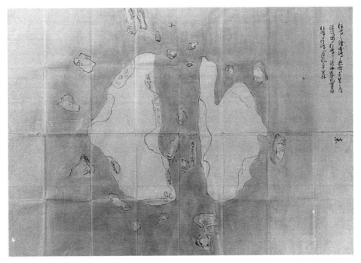

"Illustration of Matsushima" (photo of the illustration owned by the Murakawa family, property of Yonago Municipal Historical Museum)

but an old photo of it is held by the Yonago Municipal Historical Museum), that around this time the Murakawa family was actively engaged in hunting sea lions on Takeshima, known as Matsushima at that time. In 1637, Murakawa Ichibē's boat was caught in a storm on its way back from Takeshima, drifted in the opposite direction of Oki to Korea, and returned to Japan via Tsushima. A Tsushima Domain record from that incident says that the boat carried 314 barrels of sea lion oil, 60 sacks of sea lion carcasses, and 253 sea lion skins. The boat also carried abalone and other things, but the volumes were very small compared to the amount of sea lion–related cargo.

In 1656, Ichibē Masakiyo became the new family head, followed by Ichibē Masakatsu in 1689. It was in 1692, during

Masakatsu's time, when the Murakawa boat happened upon Koreans on Ulleungdo for the first time. Masakatsu was not on the boat himself and the person in charge was the captain named Kurobē. Kurobē was also the one in charge on the Ōya boat the following year when An Yong-bok was captured and taken to Japan. Masakatsu received notice of the travel prohibition and lost his job in 1696, but the Tottori Domain had him work as a salt wholesaler and gave him a livelihood in Yonago. The Murakawa family later did not have any male heirs and often had to adopt sons from the wealthy merchant families Atarashiya and Nakaya in Suetsugu, Matsue, who would then take the name Ichibē. A woman named Nui from the Murakawa family later married into the Ōya family during the Meiji period, so the Ōya and Murakawa families likely maintained an amicable relationship for a long time.

5

Oki and Takeshima

As I have already discussed, the *bakufu* permitted the Yonago merchants Ōya Kyūemon and Murakawa Ichibē to cross over to Ulleungdo, known as Takeshima at that time. For more than 70 years, they took turns every year traveling via Oki to Ulleungdo as well as Matsushima (present-day Takeshima), which they soon discovered. Here, I would like to introduce the stopover, Oki.

The Ōya and Murakawa boats, having prepared for the voyage to Ulleungdo, would have waited for the wind at Kumozu, the outer port of Mihonoseki, Shimane Prefecture. They first headed out to Nishinoshima, one of the Dōzen Islands in the Oki Islands. This was because the island was home to Takuhi Shrine, whose enshrined god helps protect those at sea. Traveling to Ulleungdo in wooden sailboats was often a dangerous venture, so everyone aboard sought protection through faith.

In 1677, a retainer by the name of Saitō Toyonobu traveled around Oki and submitted *Inshū shichō gakki* (Record of Things Seen and Heard in Oki) to the Matsue Domain— although some argue that the text was edited by the author's son, Saitō Toyohito. In this record is "Chibu-gun Takuhisan engi" (Omens of Mount Takuhi in Chibu District) which states that when Murakawa Ichibē's boat went adrift at sea and the crew prayed to the god of Mount Takuhi for help, they were guided by a fishing fire and reached an inlet. This incident served to strengthen their faith in Mount Takuhi.

Having made their visit to Takuhi Shrine, the crew would have returned to their boat and headed to Fukuura in Goka on Dōgojima, the largest island in the Oki Islands. Most illustrations depicting Oki Province in the Edo period have the text "this port is good for mooring boats and those going to Takeshima [Ulleungdo] wait for good weather in this port," meaning that they checked the wind and weather at Fukuura before departing. In *Takeshima-kō* (Thoughts on Takeshima), written by the Tottori retainer Okajima Masayoshi in 1828, we find a reference to how Ōya Kyūemon's boat departed Yonago in 1666, reached Oki ten days later, and headed to Ulleungdo a little under two months after departing Yonago. The boats carried 21 people each and there would have been one or two boats going at a time. Of the crew, eight or nine were hired in Oki.

The aforementioned Ōya boat was hit by a storm on the way home, drifted to Korea, and returned to Yonago via Tsushima. According to an old document that records the names of the returnees and their family temples, there were nine people from Oki: Tarōemon, Shōsaku, Gorōsaku, Gosuke, and Hikoshichi of Jōdoji Temple and Sakusuke Jirōzaemon, Jinshichi, and Kurosuke of Mansenji Temple. They were all from the Goka area. Jōdoji Temple still exists today but Mansenji Temple has since been abandoned.

Among the Goka fishermen who were hired to fish the

waters around Ulleungdo in the Genroku period (1688–1704), there was an individual with the merchant name Itaya. An account of his experiences was later recorded in the *Chōsei Takeshima-ki* (Longevity Takeshima Chronicle) by the Shinto priest Yada Takamasa of Izumo Grand Shrine. The name, "Itaya," is the same as that for the head house of the Yawata family, who currently resides in Kumi, Oki. If there is a connection between Itaya in the Edo period and Itaya today, then it is possible that several people called Yawata, important in this context, were the descendants of the Itaya fisherman.

There is Yawata Isaburō, who crossed over to present-day Takeshima in the early Shōwa period (1926–1989) and left behind maps and diaries about the island; Yawata Katsuyoshi, who fished around Takeshima with ten others from the Hisami Fisheries Cooperative at the request of Shimane Prefecture two years after the drawing of the Syngman Rhee Line; and Yawata Shōza, who teaches children in Okinoshima-chō that Takeshima is an inherent part of Japan based off Takeshima-related documents that he has surveyed.

This merchant named Itaya was also on the Ōya boat in 1693 when An Yong-bok and Pak Eo-dun were taken to Japan. We also have a written statement signed by the boat captains Kurobē and Heibē, according to which they departed Fukuura and reached Takeshima the next day. They then left Takeshima the day after that, returned to Fukuura two days later, left for Yonago three days later, and finally returned to Yonago via Dōzen and Nagahama in Izumo.

Furthermore, the *Longevity Takeshima Chronicle* also describes how Itaya's wife and other Fukuura women reprimanded the fishermen for forcefully arresting the foreigners and treated the Koreans with hospitality. It is recorded that An Yong-bok could speak Japanese and talked with village headmen Kyūemon of Minamigata Village and Jinpachi of Kitagata Village in present-day Goka. The contents of the talk were reported to the district deputy (*gundai*), Tanabe Jinkurō, who was in charge of all of Oki, and to the governor (*daikan*) of Dōgojima, Miyoshi Heizaemon.

As previously mentioned, An Yong-bok was able to eventually return to Korea from Nagasaki via Tsushima. In 1696, An and ten others appeared in Oki once again as they were on their way to file a complaint with Tottori Domain. They disembarked from a raging sea on Kayoiura Beach in Ōku. The location of Kayoiura is indicated on the "Illustration of Ōku Harbors," which can be found among the documents of the Saitō family of Ōku (currently deposited at the Shimane Prefectural Library). The officials Takanashi Mokuzaemon

Takuhi Shrine (Nishinoshima-chō, Oki District, Shimane Prefecture)

and Kawashima Ridayū, who were dispatched by village headman Yojiemon and the governor's office in Ōku Village, treated them with hospitality. In particular, upon hearing that An Yong-bok's group only had 3 *gō* (approx. 0.5 liters) of rice, they gathered 4 *shō* and 5 *gō* (approx. 8.1 liters) of white rice in Ōku Village, despite consecutive years of bad harvests on Oki, and delivered it to them. Not long afterward, the district deputy also sent 1 *to*, 2 *shō*, and 3 *gō* (approx. 22.1 liters).

An Yong-bok's group soon departed Oki and headed to Tottori Domain. In Tottori, they first arrived at Akasakinada in Hōki and disembarked when they were greeted by a ship at Nagaobana in Inaba. They communicated in writing with the Confucian scholar Tsuji Ban'an at Aoya Sennenji Temple, but they were unable to ascertain the reason for their visit and so they were moved to a trading place outside the castle. Subsequently, it was decided on *bakufu* orders that they should be deported, and they were moved to Aoshima in Koyamaike, after which they had no choice but to depart from nearby Karo Port and go back to Korea.

It is possible that they stopped by Oki once more on their way back. The *Longevity Takeshima Chronicle* states that a Korean boat appeared at a port called Nishimura in Oki, asking for directions to Fukuura. At the port there were people who recognized An Yong-bok and Pak Eo-dun from years prior. This caused a stir and when the boat reached Fukuura, there were even more people who rejoiced over the reunion.

It is evident that the two returned to Korea via Nagasaki the first time and then Tsushima in 1693. Since they did not disembark anywhere other than Ōku when going to Japan in 1696, it can only have been on their way back to Korea on that same trip that the people of Nishimura and Fukuura met An Yong-bok a second time.

As for later events relating to Oki, Ulleungdo (Takeshima), and Matsushima (present-day Takeshima), we have the case of the sailor Hachiemon from Hamada who went to Ama in Oki in the Tenpō period (1830–1844), a time when the Japanese travel prohibition to Ulleungdo had already been in effect for over 100 years. He crossed over to Ulleungdo on three occasions in 1833, 1834, and 1835, and brought back timber. This act was discovered, after which he was arrested and executed in 1836. This was recorded by a person called Watanabe Endayū, who was likely related to the senior village headman Watanabe Sukezō of Ama, and there is also a map of Ulleungdo that he is believed to have copied from Hachiemon.

In November 2006, I went on a survey of Ulleungdo with the Takeshima Issue Research Group. I brought along Hachiemon's map of Ulleungdo and was astonished by how accurately it showed the island's shape and bearing. In 1847, more than a decade after Hachiemon's execution, a large number of foreign ships appeared around Oki. Matsue Domain, whom the *bakufu* had put in charge of Oki, strengthened defenses by placing cannons on the islands and carrying out other measures. The Matsue Domain retainer Kanamori Kensaku also reported the local situation as well as provided a map of Ulleungdo (Takeshima) and an accompanying explanatory text called the "Illustrated Guide to Takeshima" to the domain lord Naritake. I conducted a careful examination and found that Kanamori Kensaku must have used Hachiemon's map since his map was identical, including the writing around the edges.

In that same year of 1847, a French whaling ship named *Le Liancourt* was among the foreign vessels that appeared around Oki. *Le Liancourt*'s crew disembarked at Matsushima, present-day Takeshima, and thinking it was uninhabited, named it the Liancourt Rocks. Before long, present-day Takeshima started appearing on Western nautical maps as the Liancourt Rocks, while Ulleungdo became Matsushima and Takeshima came to be depicted as a phantom island further out. This caused confusion about the islands' names in the early Meiji period, but this is something I address in the supplementary figures section starting on page 165.

6

The Genroku Takeshima Incident and the Governor of Iwami Ginzan

Let us briefly go over what has beeen covered so far. More than 70 years after the Ōya and Murakawa families received permission from the Edo *bakufu* to cross over to Ulleungdo (called Takeshima then) and Matsushima (present-day Takeshima) and felled trees, hunted sea lions, and harvested abalone, they encountered Koreans on Ulleungdo in 1692. Of the Koreans whom they encountered the following year, they brought back An Yong-bok and Pak Eo-dun to Tottori, after which the *bakufu* ordered Tsushima Domain to negotiate the Ulleungdo issue with Korea over the next three years. As a result, Japanese were prohibited from going to Ulleungdo in 1696. That same year, An Yong-bok and ten others appeared in Tottori via Oki. All of these events that took place in the Genroku period are collectively referred to as the Genroku Takeshima Incident. Moreover, the incident of Hachiemon traveling to Ulleungdo in 1833, which led to his arrest and eventual execution, is referred to as the Tenpō Takeshima Incident.

Now, what I would like to address next is that the person handling the various issues that came about at the time of the Genroku Takeshima Incident was the governor of Iwami

Ginzan (silver mine), who was in charge of administrating Oki. Historically, the administration of Oki was first managed by the Horio clan, the first lords of Matsue Domain, and then by the succeeding Kyōgoku clan, who also governed the Izumo area. However, in 1638, during the early years of the so-called Matsue Matsudaira Domain, which started with Matsudaira Naomasa, it came under the direct control of the *bakufu*'s commissioner of finance (*kanjō bugyō*) but was administrated by Matsue Domain in their stead.

Nevertheless, in 1688, the *bakufu* placed it under the control of the governor of Iwami Ginzan, the *bakufu* territory adjacent to the Matsue Domain. The *Okitō-shi* (Oki Islands Gazette, published in 1933) describes this change as follows: "In the time of the shogun Tsunayoshi, in an attempt to salvage the *bakufu*'s finances, secret orders were issued to the various lords and princes, and the *bakufu* took control of their territories. Matsudaira Tsunachika also restored Oki to the *bakufu* in the twelfth month of Jōkyō 4 [1687]. During the 34 years that followed until the sixth month of Kyōhō 5 [1726], it was governed as a territory under *bakufu* control by the governor of Ōmori Ginzan in Iwami Province."

The governor of Iwami Ginzan at this time was a man named Yui Chōbē. In 1688, the representative of the Oki *kumon* (senior village headmen), a man called Rokurōemon from Inugu Village, came out from Oki by boat to greet Yui Chōbē at the governor's seat in Ōmori. They traveled from Ōura (port of Ōda City, Shimane Prefecture) to Uryū at Izumo Grand Shrine, went via Chiburijima and Nishinoshima in Dōzen, and arrived at the seat of the district deputy (temporary governor) in Yabi Village on Dōgojima. There, he concluded the formalities for relieving the Matsue Domain and then went around to inspect various locations. This is recorded in a document called *Oki oyakunin gokōtai oboe* (Memorandum on the Change of Officials in Oki).

From this point onward, the governor of Iwami Ginzan appointed a district deputy who administered all of Oki locally as well as two assisting governors (one in Dōgojima and one in Dōzen). However, it is written in *Kanchō zuihitsu* (Miscellaneous Writings about Things Seen and Heard) by Katō San'emon, the headman of Hanehigashimura in Ginzan, that there existed a rule that among the officials dispatched to Oki, the district deputy and governor of Dōgojima should be selected from among the people brought by the governor of Iwami Ginzan from Edo, while the governor of Dōzen should be selected from locally known men originally from Ginzan. Despite the considerable distance, *Kogibune mawashibumi* (Rowboat Circular) and other documents in the Saitō family collection from Ōku Village in Oki give the impression that travel between Iwami Ginzan and Oki was popular. Moreover, *Sekishū Ginzan ryōyorozu tekagami* (Various Model Cases from Ginzan of Iwami Province), a record of Iwami Ginzan, lists the yield of rice fields in Oki and the expenses necessary for Oki's administration. Documents belonging to the Abe family, who were local officials in Ginzan, also include records related to Oki. A different family of local officials, the Muneoka family, also holds illustrations called "Copied Illustrations of Oki Province."

In 1692, the governor of Iwami Ginzan changed from Yui Chōbē to Gotō Kakuemon, while Miyoshi Heizaemon became the district deputy of Oki, Tanabe Jinkurō the governor of Dōgojima, and Nakase Dan'emon the governor of Dōzen. These people were in charge of Oki in 1693 when the boat of Yonago merchant Ōya Kyūemon brought back the Koreans An Yong-bok and Pak Eo-dun after a trip to Ulleungdo via Oki. The village headmen and senior elders (ōdoshiyori) of Kitagata and Minamigata Villages near Fukuura in Oki spoke to An Yong-bok and a text reporting the contents of that conversation to Miyoshi Heizaemon and Tanabe Jinkurō still exists today. On the way to Yonago, the boat belonging to the Ōya family also stopped at Beppu on the island of Nishinoshima where the seat of the Dōzen governor was located, so I imagine that the Dōzen governor

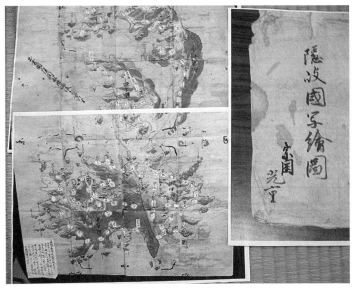

"Copied Illustrations of Oki Province" in *Muneoka-ke bunsho* (in the possession of Muneoka Mitsuaki)

Nakase Dan'emon also met the two Koreans. Most Edo-period maps depicting the area around the seat of the governor of Iwami Ginzan include a bridge called Tōjinbashi (唐人橋). Tōjin (唐人) is a general term for Koreans and Chinese but was mainly used to refer to Koreans in the San'in region. In the case of Iwami Ginzan, it is possible that there were Korean technicians doing work related to the silver mines there or that there was a place for castaway Koreans to stay.

Then, the officials of Iwami Ginzan were forced to deal with Koreans both locally and in Oki. In 1720, Iwami Ginzan's governor Takeda Kizaemon made a request for help to the *bakufu*, who then relinquished control over Oki and entrusted it to the Matsue Domain. The reason behind Takeda's request was "due to difficulties controlling Korean boats," meaning that there were difficulties in dealing with the great number of Korean ships that were now appearing at sea.

Let us now discuss the key events of the Genroku Takeshima Incident and the activities of the officials in Oki when it was under the control of the governor of Iwami Ginzan. In 1696, An Yong-bok, who had been arrested in 1693, appeared once more in Oki together with ten others. The governor of Iwami Ginzan was still Gotō Kakuemon, but the district deputy of Oki had changed to Nakase Dan'emon, the governor of Dōgojima to Matsuoka Yajiemon, and the governor of Dōzen to Yamamoto Seiemon. The district deputy Nakase Dan'emon had been the governor of Dōzen in 1693, but had been promoted. As already discussed, Oki supplied An Yong-bok's group with rice from their reserves (despite the ongoing famine) when they found out that they had little left as they were making their way to Tottori Domain. The *Annals of King Sukjong* also inform us that An Yong-bok, upon his return to Korea, related that "the lord of Oki contacted Hakushū [Tottori Domain] for us." I suspect that the person who ordered the provision of rice and the person described as the lord of Oki was Nakase Dan'emon. Soon after, the actions of An Yong-bok were reported to the Iwami governor's seat in the names of Nakase Dan'emon and Dōgojima governor Matsuoka Yajiemon. The report was carried by the Dōzen governor Yamamoto Seiemon, and a document called *Genroku 9 hinoene no toshi Chōsenbune chakugan ikkan no oboegaki* (Memorandum on the Arrival of a Korean Boat in Genroku 9 [1696] Volume 1) belonging to the Murakami Sukekurō family of Ama-chō in Oki appears to be a copy of that report. The original report submitted to the governor's seat has yet to be found.

I was delighted when the Iwami Ginzan Silver Mine was registered as a World Heritage Site in 2007 and would be properly preserved. I am certain that research on Iwami Ginzan will deepen, and I hope that we can further examine the history of how Oki was governed by people in Iwami Ginzan and other related topics.

7

The Korean Goodwill Missions
and the Takeshima Issue

The Korean goodwill missions, or embassies, were diplomatic missions from Korea to Japan. A number of these came to Japan during the Muromachi period, but it generally refers to the 12 times Korean diplomatic missions were invited to Japan for the sake of building amicable relations between the Edo *bakufu* and the Joseon kingdom following Toyotomi Hideyoshi's War of Bunroku-Keichō from 1592–1598 (known in Korea as the Japanese disturbances of the Imjin and Jeongyu years). The first mission consisted of 467 members and departed Korea in 1607. Matsuda Kō has written an article on general trends in the Korean embassies, outlining them as follows:

The Korean missions were led by the so-called three envoys, namely the *jeongsa* (envoy), the *busa* (deputy envoy), and the *jongsagwan* (chargé d'affaires) and consisted of more than 400 people who departed from the capital Hanseong, boarded ships at Busan Port, traveled via Tsushima, Iki, and Aijima, traversed the Seto Inland Sea from Shimonoseki, and disembarked at Osaka. This was the regular route, yet as there were no steamships back then, they had to rely on their sails and nothing else. Thus, it was common for the journey from Busan Port to Osaka to take forty to fifty days as they experienced countless hardships, such as storms or rough seas blocking their path. They sojourned in Osaka for three or four days, left a small number of people behind, and then traveled up Yodo River by boat and stayed in Kyoto. This was for another three or four days. Since this was their itinerary, they spent almost all day aboard boats after leaving Busan, with no chance of even smelling the scent of soil. Sometime after leaving Kyoto, they traveled on land, passed through Ōsaka-no-seki, entered Ōmi Highway, and for the first time experienced the emotion that comes with encountering the nature of Japan.

In 1617, when the second Korean embassy, 428 men strong, arrived in Japan, the chargé d'affaires Yi Seongmun spoke about the Ulleungdo (Takeshima) issue with the elder (*rōjū*) Doi Toshikatsu at Fushimi Castle in Kyoto. He said, "Japanese people came to Isotakeshima [Isotakeshima was also another name for Ulleungdo during this period] in the time of Toyotomi Hideyoshi, cut down trees and presented some of the wood to Toyotomi. He was pleased with this and bestowed the person in charge with the name Isotake Yazaemon. There are Japanese people on Isotakeshima to this day." Doi Toshikatsu was surprised to hear this and ordered Tsushima Domain to investigate. We find in *Taishū hennen-ryaku* (Abbreviated Chronology of Tsushima), a record from Tsushima Domain, that Tsushima searched the island in 1620, where they arrested and sent to Kyoto the two men

Isotake Yazaemon and his son Niemon. Yazaemon had chanced upon Ulleungdo in the late sixteenth century and had been granted permission to travel there while Japan was under the rule of Toyotomi Hideyoshi. After the death of Toyotomi in 1598 and the founding of the Edo *bakufu* under Tokugawa Ieyasu, Yazaemon had failed to seek the permission of the *bakufu* to travel to Ulleungdo. The same events are recorded in *Tsūkō ichiran* (Survey of Intercourse), a text on Japanese diplomacy in that period. Tsushima Domain took an interest in the island and requested that Korea allow them to possess it, but this was never realized.

In 1643, the fifth embassy of 462 people came to Japan to

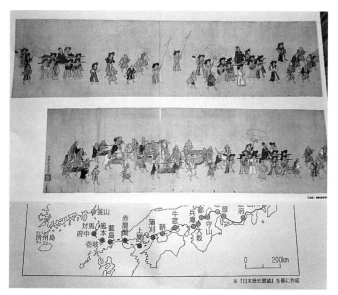

Illustrations of the Korean embassy procession and their travel route (in private possession)

List of Korean Goodwill Missions in the Edo Period

Gregorian Calendar	Korean Year	Japanese Year	Envoy	Mission	Total number of people * Those in brackets remained in Osaka
1607	Seonjo 40	Keichō 12	Yeo U-gil	Friendship	467
1617	Gwanghaegun 9	Genna 3	O Yun-gyeom	Offering congratulations on the suppression of Osaka and unification of Japan	428 (78)
1624	Injo 2	Kan'ei 1	Jeong Rip	Succession of Iemitsu	300
1636	Injo 14	Kan'ei 13	Im Gwang	Celebrating peace	475
1643	Injo 21	Kan'ei 20	Yun Sunji	Birth of Ietsuna	462
1655	Hyojong 6	Meireki 1	Jo Hyeong	Succession of Ietsuna	488 (103)
1682	Sukjong 8	Tenna 2	Yun Jiwan	Succession of Tsunayoshi	475 (112)
1711	Sukjong 37	Shōtoku 1	Jo Tae-eok	Succession of Ienobu	500 (129)
1719	Sukjong 45	Kyōhō 4	Hong Chi-jung	Succession of Yoshimune	475 (109)
1748	Yeongjo 24	Enkyō 5 (Kan'en 1)	Hong Gye-hui	Succession of Ieshige	475 (83)
1764	Yeongjo 40	Hōreki 14 (Meiwa 1)	Jo Eom	Succession of Ieharu	472 (106)
1811	Sunjo 11	Bunka 8	Kim Igyo	Succession of Ienari	336

Source: Sugihara Takashi, "Chōsen tsūshinshi to Un-Seki shohan no futan" [The Korean Goodwill Missions and the Burden on Izumo and Iwami Domains], *San'in shidan* 17 (1981)

celebrate the birth of Tokugawa Ietsuna. One of the members was official littérateur (*jesulgwan*) Pak Angi. The official littérateur was a post tasked with interacting and exchanging Chinese poetry with cultured Japanese individuals as well as answering questions about culture in a broad sense. During their stay, Pak Angi met with the Neo-Confucian scholar Hayashi Razan (also known as Dōshun) on an almost daily basis. As Pak Angi was returning to Korea, Razan gifted him the book *Nihon kokki* (History of Japan), compiled by his son Hayashi Gahō (also known as Shunsai) and others. The book describes the provinces in Japan and has the following lines about Oki Province: "There is an island called Takeshima in the sea of Oki. It is rich in bamboo and abalone. The abalone is exquisite. There are also marine animals called sea lions." Takeshima in this period referred to Ulleungdo, so we can see that the central figures in the *bakufu* considered Ulleungdo as belonging to Oki Province. In this period, the Ōya and Murakawa families were bringing back large volumes of abalone from Ulleungdo and present-day Takeshima, then known as Matsushima. They sent these to the shogun and *bakufu* ministers in Edo, so the comment "exquisite" would have come from personal experience.

There were always some members of every Korean goodwill mission who left behind records of their experiences, such as *Record of Observations in Japan* or *Record of Japan*. In 1655, a Korean goodwill mission of 488 people came to Japan to congratulate Tokugawa Ietsuna on becoming the new shogun. The *Separate Record of Observations*, written by a member called Nam Yingik, states, "Oki Province is located in the north sea; to the west, it is near Mishima and

Korean Ulleungdo." This tells us that they considered Ulleungdo as Korean territory.

Moreover, Secretary Seong Daejung, one of the 472 members in the goodwill mission of 1764, which congratulated the succession of shogun Ieharu, wrote the aforementioned *Record of Japan*. Seong Daejung's depiction of Japan from a broad perspective is to be recognized, but we must also note that there is a text called "About An Yong-bok" at the end of the volume. After An Yong-bok went to Japan twice, his account was included in the *Annals of King Sukjong*, which was compiled in 1728. Seong Daejung's *Record of Japan* has about the same contents as the *Annals of King Sukjong*, discussing Ullengdo (Takeshima), Matsushima (present-day Takeshima), and Hōki Province as well as what An Yong-bok told the Japanese.

Why did Seong Daejung write about An Yong-bok in a record of his own stay in Japan 37 years after the publication of the *Annals of King Sukjong*? Perhaps he was reminiscing about a fellow Korean who crossed the sea to Japan before him, or perhaps An Yong-bok's actions gave him a premonition about the so-called Takeshima Dispute that would later appear between Japan and Korea.

Additionally, there are many more historical facts related to local history and the Korean goodwill missions. For further reading, please see the references for this section.

8

The Japanese Sea Lion
and Takeshima

The Japanese sea lion was a species of seal known to have existed during the Edo, Meiji, Taishō (1912–1926), and Shōwa periods. It is currently thought to be extinct and only about ten stuffed specimens remain in the world. Colonies of such sea lions lived on Ulleungdo and present-day Takeshima until around 1954.

They were hunted by people from the Yonago merchant families Ōya and Murakawa, who crossed over to these islands during the Edo period. Their skin was used as well, but most sought after was their oil, which was extracted by boiling their carcasses in cauldrons. It has been written that "several *to* of oil can be extracted from one animal," and since 1 *to* equals 10 *shō* (approx. 18 liters), we can assume that they yielded quite a lot of oil. A carpenter accompanied the fishermen to the islands and built tubs there, which were used to store the oil. In 1666, a boat belonging to the Ōya family was on its way back to Yonago via Oki but was hit by a storm and drifted to Korea. The record says that that boat carried more than 300 barrels of oil.

The Murakawa family was especially active in catching Japanese sea lion on present-day Takeshima. We can get a picture of the Murakawa family's hunt from this sentence in a letter: "When one shoots sea lions on Matsushima [present-day Takeshima], the rest escape to Takeshima [Ulleungdo] and are caught there." We also have a record of one of their boats hitting a reef near Takeshima and being badly damaged. Moreover, the Murakawa family holds a detailed illustration that only depicts Takeshima, although labelled as Matsushima.

In the Edo period, the Japanese sea lion was called *michi* or *michinouo*. It is written that Shinto ritual, *ainame*, held at Izumo Grand Shrine, should be "conducted by placing an offering of food atop the skin of a *michi*." The term *michi* remains in use at shrines with a long history.

Sea lion hunting continued into the Meiji period. Nakai Yōzaburō ran a variety of businesses in Oki, such as sea cucumber fishing, and hunted sea lions on present-day Takeshima together with Ohara Iwazō and others from the same village as him from 1903, after which he went to Tokyo to ask the government to take clear possession of the island. The result was that the island fell under the jurisdiction of the governor of the Oki Islands in Shimane Prefecture on February 22, 1905. In that same year, Nakai Yōzaburō and his companions established the Takeshima Fishing and Hunting Limited Partnership Company, received permission from the prefectural government, and started hunting sea lions. They captured about 1,300 in 1906, about 2,000 in 1907, and about 1,800 in 1908.

After Takeshima was incorporated into Shimane Prefecture, the prefectural governor Matsunaga Bukichi went to the island with several prefectural staff members in August

1905, bringing back three live sea lions. Newspapers from that time report that these sea lions later died and were stuffed. The whereabouts of those stuffed specimens were long unknown, but we now know that they are kept at Izumo High School, Taisha High School, and Matsue Kita High School. An analysis by Inoue Takao, anatomy professor at the Faculty of Medicine, Tottori University, has shown that they are indeed Japanese sea lions and would have been alive around that time. We currently know of a total of seven stuffed Japanese sea lions inside Japan, including one at Shimane University and three at Tennoji Zoo in Osaka. Three were also brought back to the Netherlands by Philipp Franz von Siebold who came to Nagasaki at the end of the Edo period, which are now in Leiden and elsewhere.

There was a man called Nakawatase Jinsuke who hunted sea lions on behalf of Nakai Yōzaburō for more than thirty years during the Meiji period. He was a master hunter who

Illustration of a sea lion (*Ōya Family Documents*)
(in the possession of Shimane Prefecture Takeshima Reference Room)

Stuffed Japanese sea lion (located at Shimane Prefectural Izumo High School)

shot sea lions with a rifle from atop the reefs around Takeshima. He was on Takeshima on May 27–28, 1905, from where he witnessed the Battle of Tsushima up close during the Russo-Japanese War.

At the start of the Shōwa period, live sea lions became sought after by circuses, and Oki fishermen started capturing them by setting up nets outside caves on Takeshima and chasing them out. Yoshiyama Takeshi, who participated in such hunts, explained that capturing adult sea lions during the cub-rearing season was both strenuous and dangerous. He was 96 years old at the time of this explanation and has since passed away. Hashioka Tadashige, who was asked to capture thirty live sea lions in 1935, had a contract that paid him 140 yen per sea lion if he brought them to Sakai Port alive. Back then 100 yen was roughly equivalent to about 50,000–60,000 yen today, so it was a valuable exchange.

It seems that sea lions from Takeshima also appeared around the Oki Islands, some 158 km away, in the early Shōwa period. Yawata Shōzō, a resident of Okinoshima-chō born in 1928, explained that sea lions appeared as he was swimming in the ocean and swam with him. They even followed him up onto land back to his home after he fed them fish, remarking that they were quite friendly. Mano Takao of Nishinoshima-chō also stated that he frequently saw them at a port called Mitabe.

An essay published in South Korea criticized, among other things, Japanese overhunting for causing the extinction of the Japanese sea lion around 1945. However, everyone from the fisheries class at Sakai High School who went to Takeshima in November of 1951 testified that there were sea lions swimming alongside the boat. Testimonies to the presence of Japanese sea lions were likewise given by everyone from the fisheries class at Oki High School who visited Takeshima in June of 1953 and by the members of Kumi Fishermen's Cooperative who were fishing around Takeshima in 1954.

9

After the Travel Prohibition

Following the taking of An Yong-bok and Pak Eo-dun to Tottori Domain in 1693, the Edo *bakufu* ordered Tsushima Domain to hold diplomatic negotiations with Korea regarding Ulleungdo, which lasted three years. The former lord of Tsushima Domain, Sō Yoshizane reported that the negotiations had run into trouble, upon which the *bakufu* confirmed the status of Ulleungdo with Tottori and Matsue Domains and decided on a travel prohibition in 1696. Sō Yoshizane of Tsushima Domain was notified of the travel prohibition, and Yoshida Heima, Tottori Domain's representative (*rusui*) in Edo, was summoned to the house of the elder Toda Yamashiro-no-kami, where he received an order of the travel prohibition dated the twenty-eighth day of the first month in that same year.

According to the text *Isotakeshima jiryaku* (Abbreviated Matters of Isotakeshima), Tottori Domain collected all of the issued travel permits and submitted them to the *bakufu* shortly after receiving the order. In the spring of 1696, An Yong-bok returned to Japan with ten others; first in Oki, then in Tottori a month latter. After returning to Korea, he gave an account of his travels, which was recorded in the

Annals of King Sukjong. There he says that they went to Japan in pursuit of a group of Japanese fishermen who had been fishing around Ulleungdo (Takeshima) and Matsushima (present-day Takeshima). As the *bakufu* had prohibited travel and Tottori Domain had already returned their travel permits to the *bakufu*, it is unlikely that Japanese were fishing in those waters at that time. A careful examination of primary sources on the administration of Tottori Domain at Tottori Prefectural Museum also did not reveal any record of travel in 1696, as reported in the *Takeshima mondai ni kansuru chōsa kenkyū: Saishū hōkokusho* (Investigation Research on the Takeshima Issue: Final Report).

So, what happened to travel to Ulleungdo after the prohibition order? Numerous illustrations of Oki Province made after the prohibition include a note regarding travel to Ulleungdo (Takeshima) from Fukuura (see p. 33). In the seventy-plus years prior to the prohibition, around eight or nine Oki residents hired by the Ōya and Murakawa families went to Ulleungdo every year, so it is possible that these men, thoroughly familiar with the sea route, continued to go out fish-

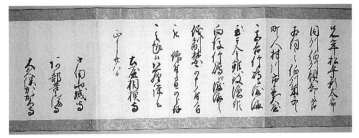

Copy of the "travel prohibition" order that reached Tottori Domain
(in the possession of Yonago Municipal Historical Museum)

ing, perhaps not to Ulleungdo (then Takeshima) but at least to Matsushima (present-day Takeshima). Yet we currently have no sources confirming this. Furthermore, Mori Katsumi, a renowned scholar of the history of Japanese-Korean interactions, wrote the following in an article titled "Kinsei ni okeru Tai-Sen mitsubōeki to Tsushima-han" (Tsushima-Korea Smuggling and Tsushima Domain in the Early-Modern Period): "Tsushima Domain took the initiative to crack down on smuggling, and at the same time, it borrowed the power of the *bakufu*. An example of this is that the *bakufu* prohibited people from Matsue Domain crossing over from Tsushima to Takeshima [Ulleungdo] around the time of the Kyōhō period." However, nothing in Mori's source, *Nagasaki-ken Minami Takagi-gun Kamishiro-mura Nabeshima-ke monjo* (Nabeshima Family Documents from Kamishiro Village, Minami Takagi District, Nagasaki Prefecture), has been found that suggests this was actually the case.

In 1833, Hachiemon from Hamada was passing by Ulleungdo and Matsushima (present-day Takeshima) in his boat as he transported goods in the direction of Echigo when he was impressed by the abundant resources of Ulleungdo. Hachiemon received informal consent from Okada Tanomo, a chief retainer (*karō*) of Hamada Domain, to travel to Ulleungdo under the pretext of going to Matsushima with the intent of boosting domanial finances. He departed from Oki and it was conventionally thought that he only did this once in 1833, but a man called Watanabe Endayū from Ama wrote that Hachiemon came to Oki in 1833, 1834, and 1835, so we may surmise that he made the trip on multiple occasions. The actions of Hachiemon were soon uncovered, and he was arrested and questioned at the Osaka magistrate's office in 1836. The chief retainer Okada Tanomo in Hamada Domain committed seppuku as he felt responsible, and implicated people were arrested one after the other. Hachiemon was transferred to Edo where he was subjected to harsh investigation followed by execution.

In 1836, when Hachiemon was arrested and questioned, there was a nineteen-year-old man who was traveling on the Iwami Road in the San'in region, asking the owners of inns about Ulleungdo (Takeshima) and making a pilgrimage to the Takatsu Kakinomoto Shrine in Masuda. This young man was Matsuura Takeshirō from Sugawa Village in Ise Province (present-day Matsusaka City, Mie Prefecture). During the Bunsei period (1818–1831) as many as 5 million people out of Japan's population of 30 million are said to have made the pilgrimage (*okagemairi*) to Ise Grand Shrine. Takeshirō grew up on the Ise Highway, met people from all over the country, and took an interest in knowing more about the rest of Japan. He studied for three years at a private school ran by Tsu Domain scholar Hiramatsu Rakusai and broadened his thinking, after which he set out on an educational journey across Japan when he was sixteen years old. In particular, Takeshirō traveled around Hokkaido on foot and regularly reported on the conditions there and on the lives of the many Ainu people. He also had an interest in the northern territories and the Russian expansion.

What astonished Takeshirō in particular were the military actions of Britain against the Chinese Qing dynasty in the First Opium War in 1840, usurping Hong Kong and forcing the opening of five ports, including Guangzhou. He was worried by the prospect of Britain advancing further east. He wrote, among other things, "Last summer, foreign ships [American and Russian barbarians] were stopping in the east and west, causing worry about the affairs of the nation." He also paid attention to Ulleungdo (Takeshima), writing, "Takeshima is located between us and Korea. It is uninhabited so foreign ships congregate there, and if they were to appear at San'in ports, the damage caused will not be slight," and "Compared to Ezo, Karafuto, and the Izu Islands, Takeshima is not very well known." Eventually, he started making brochures with the purpose of informing people about Ulleungdo (Takeshima), distributing them to intellectuals and patriots. They were all titled *Takeshima zasshi* (Takeshima Magazine), but he changed the characters used in the printing, giving them different-looking titles in 1854 (他計甚麼雑誌), 1864 (多気甚麼雑誌), and 1870 (竹島雑誌). Takeshirō argued that patriots should go to Ulleungdo, cultivate it in peacetime, and defend it as a Japanese front line in emergencies. He also thought, "There is no plan better than if patriotic men cross over to that place, engage with foreign ships in earnest, and find out what is happening in the world."

Takeshirō had many friends, and one of them was Yoshida Shōin. Among the letters left behind by Yoshida Shōin, there are those that assent to Takeshirō's call to cultivate Ulleungdo. In 1858, discussions about Ulleungdo also started at the Shōkasonjuku Academy in Hagi, Chōshū Domain because of the influence of Shōin. In 1860, Katsura Kogorō (later taking the name Kido Takayoshi) and Murata Zōroku (later Ōmura Masujirō), students at the Shōkasonjuku Academy, jointly submitted *Takeshima kaitaku negai* (Proposal for the

Cultivation of Takeshima [Ulleungdo]) to the *bakufu*, which began with the words "Takeshima [Ulleungdo] is to the northeast of Hagi, Chōshū Province." However, the cultivation of Ulleungdo proposed by Matsuura Takeshirō and planned by the retainers of Chōshū Domain in this turbulent period of treaties of amity and commerce with foreign countries from the end of the Edo period into the Meiji Restoration was never realized. Takeshirō remained interested in this area of the sea until his death at age seventy-one in 1888.

The three versions of *Takeshima Magazine* made by Matsuura Takeshirō cite various other sources, and one especially representative source is *Takeshima zusetsu* (Illustrated Guide to Takeshima) by Kanamori Kensaku. Kensaku was from Bitchū and a scholar well versed in Western matters, and according to the *Resshi roku* (Record of Upright Men) which records the careers and accomplishments of retainers of the Matsue Domain, he served the Matsue Domain as a teacher of Dutch studies. In 1849, a large number of foreign ships appeared around Oki. This was before Matthew C. Perry showed up at Uraga in 1853. Matsue Domain fortified Oki by deploying cannons and stationing retainers there.

At this tense time, Kensaku submitted the *Illustrated Guide to Takeshima*, consisting of a map and accompanying commentary, to his lord Matsudaira Naritake. Illustrations of Ulleungdo (Takeshima) closely resembling the original can be found at the National Archives of Japan in Tokyo and at the Yonago Municipal Historical Museum. In the preface of the *Illustrated Guide to Takeshima*, Kensaku writes about this illustration of Ulleungdo (Takeshima) that he himself made and submitted to the lord. Yet it has been shown that topographical and other explanations written on the map are exactly the same as those on the map drawn by Hachiemon who was executed 14 years earlier. It is my suspicion that Kensaku took this map and left it for posterity in his own name as he thought it could never see the light of day under the name of the executed criminal Hachiemon. The three versions of *Takeshima Magazine* by Matsuura Takeshirō also all contain maps of Ulleungdo (Takeshima). Since he cites the illustration of Kensaku, the text there also comes from Hachiemon.

Due to a dearth of sources pertaining to Hachiemon, Kensaku, and Matsuura Takeshirō who took an interest in Ulleungdo (Takeshima) following the prohibition of travel to the island, research remains insufficient, but I look forward to the discovery of new sources and further research.

10

Matsushima Becomes
Liancourt (Lianco) Island

As discussed thus far, present-day Ulleungdo was referred to as Takeshima and present-day Takeshima as Matsushima in Edo-period Japan. This changed at the end of the Edo period into the early Meiji period when Ulleungdo became Matsushima and Matsushima became Liancourt Island, Liancourt Rocks being the English name for present-day Takeshima. The background for these changes was a growing awareness of Asia in America and Europe and later whaling in vast swathes of ocean, which necessitated the local procurement of firewood and water in distant seas.

Amid this, foreign ships also increasingly started appearing in the Sea of Japan. First, we have a French naval ship passing by Ulleungdo in 1787, which resulted in Ulleungdo being named Dagelet Island by French explorer Jean-François de Galaup, comte de La Pérouse. Next was the *Argonaut*, a British ship, that "discovered" Ulleungdo in 1789. This led to British explorer James Colnett naming the island Argonaut Island after the ship. It was the same island (Ulleungdo), but because the two countries had measured longitude and latitude differently, European sea charts came to show two separate islands: Argonaut Island closer to Korea to the west and Dagelet Island to the east.

A new reaction to these two islands in the Sea of Japan was shown by the German physician Philipp Franz von Siebold. He came to Japan in 1823, worked as a physician at the trading post in Nagasaki, and was given a residence in Narutaki outside Nagasaki where he treated Japanese and taught them medicine, training Takano Chōei and many others as his students. He was also ordered to study the nature of Japan and conduct humanities research there, acquiring vast volumes of materials with the help of many Japanese friends and students said to number more than one hundred people. In 1828, when his return to Europe was drawing near, it was discovered that *bakufu* astronomer Takahashi Sakuzaemon had gifted von Siebold with several maps of Japan, including the Inō maps that were prohibited from being taken out of the country. Sakuzaemon was arrested and died in prison. Von Siebold was also put under house arrest in Dejima for one year and deported in 1829. (He would later come back to Japan as an advisor of the Dutch Trading Company.)

Back in the Netherlands, he began writing *Nippon*, said to be the most extensive compilation of knowledge about Japan in those days. He speculated and wrote that Argonaut Island on maps circulating in Europe was what the Japanese called Takeshima (he actually misspelled Takeshima as "Takasima") and that Dagelet Island was Matsushima. When I went to the Nagasaki Museum of History and Culture, I measured von Siebold's map of Japan and found that it was 63 cm high and 83 cm wide and made in 1840.

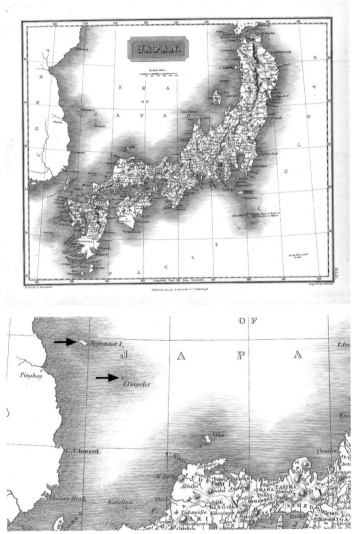

A European sea chart showing Ulleungdo as the two islands, Argonaut and Dagelet (in private possession)

Later in 1849, a large number of foreign ships started appearing around the Oki Islands. On the eighteenth day of the second month of that year, a large foreign ship appeared at Mitabe, Nishinoshima-chō, and 16 people disembarked. Four days later, two more foreign ships appeared at Oki, Okinoshima-chō. In the third month, even more ships appeared one after the other. Matsue Domain, under orders from the Edo *bakufu*, dispatched retainers and increased defenses in Oki.

There was a ship that approached present-day Takeshima in 1849 as well. It was the French whaler *Le Liancourt*. They viewed the island as a discovery and gave it the name Liancourt Island or Liancourt Rocks. Not long after, this new name started appearing on European sea charts alongside Argonaut and Dagelet. Russian and British ships also approached present-day Takeshima and gave it their own names, but these other names hold little historical significance. European sea charts and maps depicting Argonaut, Dagelet, and Liancourt as three different islands were brought to Japan, resulting in *Dai Nihonkoku enkai ryakuzu* (Concise Map of the Seas around Japan) (Keiō 3 [1867]), edited by Katsu Kaishū, also showing these three as islands between the Korean Peninsula and the Oki Islands, going from west to east.

However, the issue here is Argonaut Island, which was meant to depict present-day Ulleungdo but was mischarted and thus shown in a fictitious location on maps. When the Russian warship *Pallada* conducted a detailed survey of Ulleungdo and its surroundings in 1854, it reported that Argonaut Island did not exist. As a result, European sea charts and maps started indicating the location with dotted lines or the text "no longer in existence," soon leaving it out completely. With the disappearance of Argonaut Island, the name Takeshima also disappeared, and Ulleungdo became established as "Dagelet Island, also known as Matsushima."

Later, Liancourt Island became the established name for present-day Takeshima. The name was also corrupted and shortened so that it sometimes was given as Lianco Island. In 1904, Nakai Yōzaburō submitted to the Japanese government a "Request for the Territorial Incorporation and Lease of Lianco Island." There, he wrote, "There is an uninhabited island commonly called Lianco Island in the distant seas 55 *ri* [approx. 216 km] southeast of Korean Ulleungdo." When I discussed Takeshima with the elders of Okinoshima-chō, I often heard pronunciations similar in sound to "Lianco Island."

Having received Nakai Yōzaburō's request, the government approached Shimane Prefecture for consultation. In turn, Shimane Prefecture asked Higashi Bunsuke, the governor of the Oki Islands, about his opinions on the possibilities of administrating the island, the island's name, and other matters. Higashi Bunsuke responded, "There is nothing to stop the island from being placed under the jurisdiction of the Oki Islands if it is incorporated into Japan, and I believe Takeshima is the appropriate name." His reason for the name Takeshima was that both Takeshima and Matsushima were the names used during the Edo period, but since Ulleungdo had come to be known as Matsushima, Takeshima should be used for Liancourt (Lianco) Island as the name was no longer used due to a misnaming. This answer was relayed from Shimane Prefecture to the government, who made a cabinet decision on the territorial incorporation of this island in January 1905. Thus, Liancourt Island became a part of Shimane Prefecture and was officially named and recognized as Takeshima in Japan.

11

The Tenpō Takeshima Incident
and Hachiemon

Now I will talk in detail about some events that took place during the Tenpō years (1830–1844) that are collectively known as the Tenpō Takeshima Incident.

Hachiemon, who was introduced earlier, owned a cargo ship in Matsubaraura, Hamada Domain in the Iwami area of Shimane Prefecture. He was both the owner and captain of the boat. It was conventionally thought that his merchant name was Aizuya, but according to an investigation by Morisu Kazuo, a researcher living in Hamada City, where he mainly looked at the cargo ship registers of ports visited by Hachiemon and local documents, it was actually Imazuya. Hachiemon frequently transported cargo to Matsumae in Hokkaido, passing by Ulleungdo (Takeshima) with its abundant nature and fish-rich waters. Some of the routes of the *kitamaebune* (Edo- and Meiji-period cargo ships in the Sea of Japan) going between Hokkaido and Shimonoseki went through Ulleungdo and Matsushima (present-day Takeshima). We know this from the *Iwami External Record* from Hamada Domain, sailors' stories recorded by the Ezo explorer Kondō Jūzō, and maps belonging to Takadaya Kahē.

The finances of Hamada Domain were strained at the

time and when Hachiemon found out about this, he approached the accountant Hashimoto Sanbē. Speaking to Hashimoto, he told him "The domain would profit if we go to Takeshima, log the naturally neglected bamboo, and bring back the marine products," "Takeshima is unmarked on all maps I've seen and not colored as Korean, so I think the island belongs to no one," and "If I were to lose my life in the service of my province, then I'd die gladly." This is written in Morisu Kazuo's *Hachiemon to sono jidai* (Hachiemon and His Time). Others who also became involved in this venture were Okada Tanomo, a chief retainer (*karō*) of Hamada Domain, and Matsui Zusho, a senior local official. Finally, the approval of the domain lord Matsudaira Suō-no-kami Yasutō was needed. At the time, Yasutō held the important post of chief elder (*hittō rōjū*) in the *bakufu* and lived in Edo. It did not take long for a response hinting at the approval of travel to come from the domain's Edo residence, a response along the lines of "It is difficult to establish Takeshima [Ulleungdo] as Japanese land, so how about Matsushima [present-day Takeshima]?" and "Products brought back must not be circulated east of Osaka."

With this, Hachiemon started making plans to cross over to Ulleungdo under the pretense of going to Matsushima (present-day Takeshima). In 1833, a party of eight sailors, consisting of Hachiemon, the financier Awajiya Zenbē, Shigesuke, Shinbē, Kumezō, Otogorō, Yasukichi, and Shinsaku departed from Hamada. They headed straight for Ulleungdo but drifted to Mishima in Chōshū due to strong winds and bad weather. They had no choice but to go east along the coast, cross over to Oki, and stop at Fukuura, the base from which the Ōya and Murakawa families had gone to Ulleungdo (Takeshima) for more than 70 years. They waited for good wind, departed Fukuura and first sighted Matsushima, but since they knew it was made up of mostly reef, they did not disembark, and continued on to Ulleungdo which they reached four days later. When they made landfall, there was a large number of sea lions swimming in the waters around the island. After disembarking, they entered the forest and were attacked by large birds. They shot the birds and one sea lion, which they then brought back with them.

They felled 40–50 big trees, including zelkovas and paulownias, as well as collected what was likely Korean ginseng. Along with harvesting resources from the island, Hachiemon used a compass to repeatedly circle the island and made a detailed map for the sake of future development. The *Takeshima tokai ikkenki zen* (Complete Record of the Takeshima Travel Incident) is a record of testimonies collected during the interrogations that followed the uncovering of this expedition. It contains the text "All of us traveled around all four sides of the island and used a compass I had brought to carefully track the directions" and "I personally drew the shape of the island as a map." This map by Hachiemon has yet to be found, but we have found two maps said to be copies of it.

They departed from Ulleungdo over two months later and headed directly for Hamada, but the sea was rough. They dumped the large birds, sea lion, and even some of the timber into the sea, fearful that they had angered a god by killing the animals. They finally managed to make it back on the twenty-seventh day of the same month.

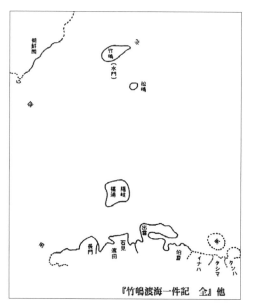

Map included in *Takeshima tokai ikkenki zen* (in the possession of the University of Tokyo, General Library) Reproduced from Morisu Kazuo, *Hachiemon to sono jidai* (Hamada: Hamada City Board of Education, 2002)

Going back to the copies of the map by Hachiemon, we have one with the text "I was allowed to copy it on the night of the nineteenth day of the eleventh month, Tenpō 4 [1833]; the owner Gonkichi." We also have a map drawn by Watanabe Endayū of Ama in Oki with the text "Hachiemon crossed over to Takeshima via Oki in Tenpō 4 [1833], 5 [1834], and 6 [1835], so I copied it in Tenpō 6 [1836]."

In 2006, I helped survey Ulleungdo and compared the island's topography and so forth with those of the two maps. I found that the shapes of the current island and surrounding reefs were exactly the same and was surprised by the accuracy of Hachiemon's drawing. Furthermore, although it had previously been thought that Hachiemon went once in 1833, the discovery of these maps has shown that he went at least three times.

The central *bakufu* found out about Hachiemon's unauthorized travels in 1836. There are various theories about how this happened, but the most likely is that Mamiya Rinzō, a *bakufu* investigator conducting local inquiries, heard about them in Shimokō in Hamada and reported the violations. Hachiemon was arrested in Hamada by men dispatched by the Osaka magistrate's office and was interrogated at the magistrate's offices in both Osaka and Edo. He was "sentenced to death for his insolence" and was executed on the twenty-third day of the twelfth month of that year. He was thirty-nine years old.

The accountant Hashimoto Sanbē was likewise sentenced to death, and the chief retainer Okada Tanomo and the senior official Matsui Zusho committed suicide while the other two were interrogated. The Hamada lord and *bakufu* chief elder Matsudaira Suō-no-kami had resigned from his posts on account of illness already in 1835 but was also subject to an order requiring "retirement and strict modesty" as well as house arrest for the crime of supervisory negligence.

On the basis of this Tenpō Takeshima Incident, Matsue Domain issued a document reaffirming the travel prohibition of 1696. Notices regarding the travel prohibition were displayed in many public spaces throughout Japan.

12

Matsuura Takeshirō

Matsuura Takeshirō worked to convince people of the importance of Ulleungdo and Takeshima from the end of the Edo period through to the early Meiji period. Takeshirō was born in Sugawa Village, Ichishi District, Ise Province (present-day Matsusaka City, Mie Prefecture) in 1818. His home was on the road leading to Ise Grand Shrine, so from childhood he frequently had opportunities to see pilgrims from all over Japan. This imbued young Takeshirō with a curiosity to know more about all of Japan, so that *Nihon meisho zue* (Illustrations of Famous Places in Japan) became his favorite book to carry around.

He was also driven, leaving home at age sixteen to start traveling the country on foot. In particular, he went to Hokkaido six times, and we know that "Hokkaido" and quite a few other place names used today were given by him.

In 1836, he traveled to the San'in region, where he visited the Izumo Grand Shrine and the Takatsu Kakinomoto Shrine in Masuda, walking all the way to Hagi in Yamaguchi Prefecture. It is written in his autobiography that the owner of an inn in the Iwami area told him about the Hamada captain Chōbē who frequently traveled to Ulleungdo during the

Kyōhō era (1716–1736). The arrest and execution of Hachiemon had happened just before Takeshirō came to San'in, so it is possible that he heard about Hachiemon as well.

After this, he went around Kyushu and then to Tsushima. Takeshirō was especially concerned with the military actions of the British against the Chinese Qing dynasty during the First Opium War in 1840, where they forced open many ports. Seeing this, he also came to perceive the danger posed by more foreign ships appearing around Japan.

Takeshirō wrote and distributed a booklet called *Takeshima Magazine* in 1854. In 1864, he wrote another *Takeshima Magazine* spelled with different characters, and

Photograph of Matsuura Takeshirō (property of the Matsuura Takeshirō Memorial Museum in Matsusaka City, Mie Prefecture)

in 1870, another one. In his writings, he advocated for people to go to Ulluengdo (referred to as Takeshima at that time) and find out more about the foreign ships appearing there, in turn learning more about what was happening in the rest of the world.

Someone who answered Takeshirō's call was Yoshida Shōin from Chōshū Domain. As representatives, Katsura Kogorō and Murata Zōroku, students at Shoin's Shōkasonjuku Academy, submitted a proposal to cultivate Ulleungdo to the *bakufu* but this was never realized. In *Takeshima Magazine*, Takeshirō cites various sources, including *Illustrated Guide to Takeshima* and *Kanamori Kensaku hikki* (Writings of Kanamori Kensaku) by Kanamori Kensaku. In addition, he cites *Hōkimindan* (Folk Stories of Hōki) from Tottori Domain. Takeshirō's three booklets all contain illustrations of Ulleungdo, although slightly different in shape, but the notes describing the topography make it clear that the original map was the illustration submitted to the domain lord Matsudaira Naritake by Kanamori Kensaku in 1849.

At the same time, we can also show that Kensaku's illustration was made using an illustration by Hachiemon, who had been arrested and executed 14 years prior. In the end, the nineteen-year-old Matsuura Takeshirō who traveled to Hamada in 1836 came to inherit the map of Hachiemon via Kensaku. It feels somehow fateful.

Toward the end of his life, Takeshirō built a study using timber that he had ordered from all the places in Japan that he had traveled to and made it his daily routine to spend time there. The Senge family of Izumo Grand Shrine in the San'in region sent him wood from an old home shrine.

13

The Japanese Who Crossed over to Ulleungdo in the Early Meiji Period

Following the end of Japan's policy of national isolation after Perry's arrival in 1853 and with momentum gathering for exploring foreign lands with the birth of the new Meiji government, Japanese people once more started going to Ulleungdo, where travel had been previously prohibited. In particular, the Japan-Korea Treaty was concluded in 1876, leading to the opening of the three ports of Incheon, Busan, and Wonsan, and followed by more concrete regulations in the Japan-Korea Rules of Commerce, Regulations on the Treatment of Japanese Fishermen, and Regulations on the Trade of Japanese Nationals. With this, more and more Japanese set out to the Korean Peninsula as well as Ulleungdo and other islands to pursue business ventures. A man called Yi Kyu-won went to Ulleungdo as an investigator in 1882 to investigate the presence of Japanese on the island. On the shore, he found a wooden sign 6 *shaku* (1.8 m) long with the words "Keyakidani, Matsushima of the Japanese Empire" written in ink and signed "Erected by Iwasaki Tadateru." He also met six or seven Japanese and saw the provisional cabins they lived in.

The *Takeshima nisshi* (Takeshima Journal, written in

1971), the memoirs of a man named Yawata Saitarō, talks about a merchant whose business was named Yahoya and was a relative of Saitarō. The text mentions that this person regularly went to Korea and Ulleungdo to sell cedar bark for making roofs in the early 1890s, and that he harvested abalone at present-day Takeshima on his way home.

Around 1877, requests to develop Ulleungdo were submitted by Mutō Heigaku of Fukushima Prefecture, Saitō Shichirobē of Chiba Prefecture, Toda Takayoshi of Shimane Prefecture, and others. Sewaki Hisato, a trade official dispatched to Vladivostok by the government, advised that their requests should be approved. Moreover, an entry from December 18, 1876, in Sewaki's diary mentions that a Shimane fisherman called Shibata Tahei and six others had

Ulleungdo gamchal ilgi (Ulleungdo Investigation Diary; in the possession of Jeju National Museum)

drifted to Ulleungdo due to strong winds two or three years prior. Two of the seven lived there for three years before returning home, while the remaining five were thought to be there still. In the second decade of Meiji (ca. 1877–1886), the number of Japanese people going to Ulleungdo to commercially fell trees increased yearly. People from Yamaguchi Prefecture were especially numerous and the Yamaguchi Prefectural Archives has *Meiji 16-nen Utsuryōtō ikken-roku* (Record of the Meiji 16 [1883] Ulleungdo Incident) and many other Ulleungdo-related documents from that time.

Park Yeong-hyo, who came to Japan as part of the good-will mission to apologize for the people attacking the Japanese legation in Korea in what is known as the Imo Incident, objected to the Japanese advance into Ulleungdo. In response

Takeshima kōshō (Takeshima Investigation) (Ministry of Foreign Affairs material, in the possession of the National Archives of Japan, Digital Archive)

the Meiji government ordered each prefecture to investigate the situation.

In Yamaguchi Prefecture, a man named Yokotani Saichi wrote a report in 1883 titled *Matsushima keikyōsho* (The Situation on Matsushima), saying that about 400 Japanese were conducting commercial logging in teams of eight, with five teams consisting of people from Yamaguchi Prefecture.

The Meiji government ordered all Japanese to return home, dispatching a ship called the *Echigomaru* to Ulleungdo in October 1883. The people who happened to be on the island then numbered a total of 244, consisting of 134 from Yamaguchi Prefecture, 33 from Fukuoka, 29 from Shimane, 18 from Hiroshima, 14 from Ehime, 9 from Nagasaki, 3 from Ōita, 2 from Okayama, 1 from Tottori, and 1 from Kagoshima. They were forced to return home but did not face charges.

14

The Grand Council of State's Directive in 1877

Up until this point the story has been slightly complicated where present-day Takeshima has been referred to as Matsushima or Liancourt Island and where Ulleungdo has been called Takeshima or Matsushima. Now, I will talk about a topic that is also being hotly debated by experts on the Takeshima issue: "Takeshima and the other island have no relation to Japan," which was a statement approved by the Grand Council of State in response to an inquiry on the matter. It is one of the points of contention in the ongoing Takeshima Dispute.

This is somewhat repetitive, but present-day Ulleungdo was referred to as Takeshima and present-day Takeshima as Matsushima for most of the Edo period. In the latter half of the 1780s in the mid-Edo period, two foreign ships appeared in the Sea of Japan. One charted Ulleungdo's location and named it Dagelet Island, while the other charted it incorrectly, placed it closer to Korea, and named it Argonaut Island. This was then included in European sea charts and maps.

There was one person who saw this and subsequently caused some confusion. It was the German physician Philipp Franz von Siebold who came to Nagasaki to work at the

Dutch trading post. He taught Western studies to Takano Chōei and was the father of Japan's first female physician Kusumoto Ine through his romance with the courtesan Kusumoto Taki. After his return to Europe, he produced a map of Japan that identified Argonaut Island (also labelled as Takeshima and placed near the Korean Peninsula) and Dagelet Island (also labelled as Matsushima) further to the east. In reality, both Argonaut and Dagelet were names for the same island, Ulleungdo. This was in 1840.

Meanwhile, there was a boat that disembarked on present-day Takeshima, which had been called Matsushima since the Edo period, around this time. This was the French whaler *Le Liancourt* in 1849. They named it "Liancourt Island" before leaving. As a result, maps started appearing that depicted three islands between the Korean Peninsula and Oki: Takeshima (non-existent Ulleungdo), Matsushima (real Ulleungdo), and Liancourt Island (present-day Takeshima). A representative map that does this is the *Concise Map of the Seas around Japan*, edited by Katsu Kaishū in the last year of the Edo period, 1867.

Now, we have finally reached the Meiji period. In 1871, the Meiji government moved to abolish the domains and establish prefectures. The government had to exchange views with the new prefectures on a variety of issues. In 1876, the government's Ministry of Home Affairs (present-day Ministry of Internal Affairs and Communications) asked Shimane Prefecture about the status of Takeshima, likely because they needed to verify the land register for the land tax reform.

Shimane Prefecture responded to Home Minister Ōkubo Toshimichi on October 16, 1876, in the form of an inquiry signed by the prefectural secretary Sakai Jirō, who represented the prefectural governor Satō Nobuhiro. The main point of the inquiry submitted by Shimane Prefecture, titled *Nihonkai-nai Takeshima hoka ittō chiseki hensangata ukagai* (Inquiry about the Land Register Compilation of Takeshima and One Other Island in the Sea of Japan), was that Takeshima should be "considered part of the western San'in region," and it explained that the Ōya and Murakawa families had been crossing over to the islands since the Edo period. It is also clear that the explanation cites Ōya and Murakawa family documents. Attached is an illustration called the *Isotake-shima ryakuzu* (Rough Map of Isotakeshima), which is said to have been made based on maps from the Genroku years.

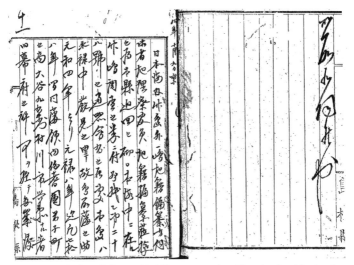

Nihonkai-nai Takeshima hoka ittō chiseki hensangata ukagai (Inquiry about the Land Register Compilation of Takeshima and One Other Island in the Sea of Japan, (*Land Register*, Meiji 9 [1876]), (in the possession of Shimane Prefecture Public Records Center)

A response to this was dispatched on April 9, 1877, in the name of Assistant Vice-Minister of Home Affairs Maejima Hisoka, who represented Ōkubo Toshimichi. It contained an instruction that can be interpreted as "Takeshima and the other island have no relation to Japan." This response was approved through a decision by the Grand Council of State, a government agency that existed at that time.

The issue here is what is meant by "Takeshima and the other island."

The approvals of the Grand Council of State from this period can be found in texts such as *Dajō ruiten* (Documents of the Grand Council of State) and *Kōbunroku* (Record of Official Documents). The text is appended to the explanatory materials submitted by Shimane Prefecture, but researchers

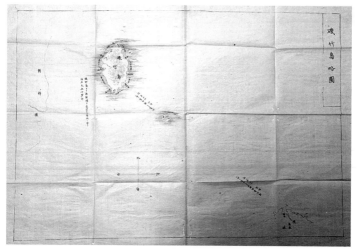

Isotakeshima ryakuzu (*Land Register*, Meiji 9 [1876], in the possession of Shimane Prefecture Public Records Center)

disagree on how it should be read. It starts off with "Isotake-shima is also called Takeshima, located 120 *ri* (approx. 470 km) northwest of Oki Province, with a total circumference of 10 *ri* (approx. 40 km), and consists of steep mountains and little level ground." Also judging from the descriptions of the island's flora and fauna, this must be present-day Ulleungdo. It goes on to say, "Next there is an island called Matsushima, with a circumference of no more than 30 *chō* [approx. 3,270 m], located on the same line as Takeshima and separated from Oki by 80 *ri* (approx. 264 km), and having few trees but yielding fish and animals. In the Eiroku period, the merchant Ōya Jinkichi from Yonago, Aimi District, Hōki Province, was sailing on his way back from Echigo but was hit by a typhoon and drifted here." Although parts of this text are incorrect, such as the period, "the other island" mentioned here is referred to as Matsushima.

The issue then becomes what "Matsushima" referred to. One interpretation it is that Matsushima was the Matsushima of the Edo period, meaning present-day Takeshima, which would point to a decision that neither Ulleungdo (Takeshima) or present-day Takeshima (Matsushima) were Japanese territory. An alternative interpretation of this passage is that since Ōya Jinkichi drifted to Ulleungdo, both Takeshima and Matsushima signify Ulleungdo, which means that the Meiji government thought it was only Ulleungdo that had nothing to do with Japan and made no reference to present-day Takeshima, which was called Liancourt Island at that time.

As I have already mentioned, a state of confusion had lasted since the end of the Edo period, where Ulleungdo was known as both Takeshima and Matsushima. We can find many references to Ulleungdo as Matsushima, especially in the early Meiji period.

In 1876, both Mutō Heigaku of Fukushima Prefecture and Saitō Shichirobē of Chiba Prefecture had submitted separate requests to conduct commercial logging (松島開拓願) on Ulleungdo (referred to as Matsushima here) to the Ministry of Foreign Affairs. In 1877, Toda Takayoshi of Shimane Prefecture submitted an application to cross over to Takeshima (竹島渡海願), where Takeshima referred to Ulleungdo. Sewaki Hisato, who had been dispatched as a trade official to Vladivostok near Ulleungdo, asked the government to accept the development applications since "Matsushima has an abundance of large trees." Park Yeong-hyo, who came to Japan leading the goodwill mission of 1882, complained to Lord of Foreign Affairs Inoue Kaoru about Japanese people going to Ulleungdo. The following year on March 31, the Ministry of Home Affairs issued the following directive to all prefectural directors: "The Japanese and Korean governments have previously agreed that Japanese should not arbitrarily set foot on the island known as Matsushima in Japan, alternatively called Takeshima, and referred to as Ulleungdo in Korea."

I explain this in my paper titled *Shimizu Jōtarō no Chōsen yochizu ni tsuite* (On Shimizu Jōtarō's Great Map of Korea), which can be found under "Investigation Results and Reports" on the Web Takeshima Issue Research Institute website. Moreover, I recently heard from another researcher that a letter titled "Inquiry Regarding the Development of Matsushima in the Sea of Japan" and signed by the Shimane prefectural governor Sakai Jirō (the prefectural secretary who submitted an inquiry to the Ministry of Home Affairs in 1876) was submitted to the Lords of Home Affairs and Agricultural Affairs. The contents were an inquiry in response to an application to develop Matsushima submitted by Ōya Kensuke from Asai Village, Naka District, Shimane Prefecture. The text makes it clear that the Matsushima mentioned here was Ulleungdo. In response to this, the Ministries of Home Affairs and Foreign Affairs exchanged some letters, and one of the individuals in charge used the words "about the matter of Takeshima and Matsushima, i.e., Ulleungdo, Korea." This meant that the island called Ulleungdo was known as both Takeshima and Matsushima.

That same year (1876), responding to a question about the historical issue of the land register, Shimane Prefecture produced and submitted an inquiry about "Takeshima and the other island" mainly on the basis of historical facts from the Edo period. The Ministry of Home Affairs responded by issuing instructions that directly copied the wording "Takeshima and the other island," but it is highly likely that the meaning was that the island [Ulleungdo] known as both Takeshima and Matsushima is not Japanese territory, which reflected the situation in the early Meiji period. Yet I am certain that further analysis of the relevant documents and maps is necessary for everyone to be convinced of this. I believe this issue is a key part of the Takeshima Dispute.

In 2009, I discovered the Ministry of Home Affairs' reply to the aforementioned Matsushima development application submitted by Ōya Kensuke and one other person in an entry from January 31, 1882, in *Kenchi yōryō* (The Outline of Prefectural Administration), which annually summarizes the administration of Shimane Prefecture in journal form. The response was that the development application could not be approved since "the matter of Matsushima is in accordance with the most recent directive," meaning that the directive of 1877 remained unchanged. Because the 1877 directive was that Takeshima and the other island (Matsushima) had no relation to Japan, this makes it clear that the Matsushima of the 1877 directive was Ulleungdo.

15

About *The Chronology of Korea*
by Mori Junzaburō

The littérateur Mori Ōgai (real name Rintarō) was from Tsu-wano, Shimane Prefecture. He was also knowledgeable about Korean history and wrote the novella *Sabashi Jingorō* on the theme of the Korean goodwill missions.

Ōgai had two younger brothers and one younger sister. His youngest brother was called Junzaburō and was seventeen years younger than him. In 1904, one year prior to present-day Takeshima becoming part of Shimane Prefecture, Junzaburō published a work called *Chōsen nenpyō* (The Chronology of Korea).

After the birth of his sister Kimiko, Junzaburō's family moved from Tsuwano to Tokyo. Junzaburō himself was born on April 15, 1879, in Mukōjima, Tokyo. After graduating junior high school in Tokyo, he enrolled at Tokyo Senmon Gakkō, which is now present-day Waseda University, in 1901 to study history. He wrote and published *The Chronology of Korea* in 1904 as a student there.

After graduating, he worked part time at the Historio-graphical Institute of Tokyo Imperial University (present-day University of Tokyo) for three years, primarily deciphering sources from the Nanboku-chō period (1337–1392) under the scholar Tanaka Yoshinari. Afterward, he started working as director of the Kyoto Prefectural Library by recommendation of Ueda Bin, professor at Kyoto Imperial University and a friend of his brother Ōgai, subsequently living in Kyoto for most of his life. In addition to his regular job, he studied history and edited various journals on the side.

He was also known as a collector of historical documents. In particular, he had more than one hundred documents related to the Korean goodwill missions, even influencing his eldest brother Ōgai. He had a strong interest in Korea and considered going there to work, but this was never realized as Ōgai opposed it on account of Junzaburō's frail health.

Now, if we turn to *The Chronology of Korea*, it is a compact book of 316 pages with an astounding number of bibliographic entries. In particular, an acquaintance named

Mori family photograph at their residence, Kanchōrō (1897); *far left*, Junzaburō, *far right*, Ōgai. (In the possession of Mori Ōgai Memorial Museum in Tsuwano, Kanoashi District, Shimane Prefecture)

Shidehara Taira, who worked as an advisor on education administration for the Korean government in Keijō (present-day Seoul), supplied him with many Korea-related materials not to be found in Japan. The preface of the book was also written by Shidehara.

The book's introduction briefly describes Korea's geography and history, while the main body of the book is a chronology divided into the three parts of Japan, Korea, and China, naming their respective era names, emperors, and kings from 57 BCE until 1903. This is followed by the "Chronology of Japanese-Korean Interactions," which describes the history of exchanges between Japan and Korea by era name. Lastly, there is a genealogy of the Sō clan of Tsushima, who had been in charge of Japanese-Korean exchanges.

What I want to highlight the most in this book is the *Chōsen zenzu* (Complete Map of Korea) that is shown in various places. Place names and such change over time, and this is especially true for the name of Ulleungdo.

The first map shows Ulleungdo as Usan. The second map has no name. Subsequently, it is shown as Ulleungdo, Takeshima, and Matsushima, in that order. The final foldout map measures 42 cm (h) x 25 cm (w) and shows it as Ulleungdo (Matsushima). None of the versions of the *Complete Map of Korea* show present-day Takeshima. This is an indication that Mori Junzaburō perceived present-day Takeshima as Japanese territory. *The Chronology of Korea* was published one year before Takeshima became part of Shimane Prefecture and indirectly informs us about various matters from that time.

Moreover, there is something I recently learned about the names for Ulleungdo from other books published around the same time as *The Chronology of Korea*. These include *Kyōkayō Kankoku ryakushi* (Abbreviated Gazette of Korea for Teaching; Shunpōsha, 1902), *Saikin Kankoku jijō yōran* (Outline of Recent Korean Affairs; Resident-General of Korea, 1909), and Noguchi Yasuoki's *Kankoku Minami Manshū* (Korea and South Manchuria; Seibidō, 1910). They call it "Ulleungdo (Usando, meaning Matsushima)," "Ulleungdo (Matsushima)," and "Ulleungdo with the Japanese name Matsushima," respectively. This reinforces the accuracy of Junzaburō's perception.

In March 1912, at the age of thirty-four, Junzaburō married Shizuko, daughter of Yonebara Tsunayoshi of Tsuwano, the Mori family's hometown. After his death at age sixty-six on March 20, 1944, Shizuko retuned to Tsuwano and spent her remaining years there.

16

The Russo-Japanese War
and Takeshima

According to Nakai Yōzaburō's reflections in his *Jigyō keiei gaiyō* (Overview of Business Management), when he went to Tokyo in 1904 to submit *Ryankotō ryōdo hennyū narabini kashisage negai* (Request for the Territorial Incorporation and Lease of Lianco Island) to the Ministries of Home, Foreign, and Agricultural Affairs, it was almost rejected as the person in charge at the Ministry of Home Affairs stated, "At this point in time [during the Russo-Japanese War], it would be a rather difficult decision with extremely little benefit to take hold of a single, tiny, and barren reef that might be Korean territory, and thereby make all foreign countries observing us suspect that we harbor ambitions to annex Korea."

It is true Nakai Yōzaburō's request came at the time of the Russo-Japanese War. The Russo-Japanese War was one of several conflicts waged among the Qing, Russia, and Japan as they sought to expand their influence to Korea. It started with clashes between Chinese and Japanese forces that were deployed to Korea under the pretext of quelling the Dong-hak Peasant Revolution, which led to the First Sino-Japanese War in 1894. In the following year, Japan was victorious and gained Taiwan and the Liaodong Peninsula under the Treaty of Shimonoseki.

In response to this, however, Russia invited Germany and France to initiate the Triple Intervention, where they advised Japan to relinquish the Liaodong Peninsula for reasons such as "Japan's advance into the Liaodong Peninsula will render Korea's independence in name only." In Japan, there were those calling for retribution against Russia, but the Meiji government asked the people to persevere in the face of hardship for the sake of long-term gain, focusing instead on building up the country's military capacities. Eventually, the

Monument to the war dead of the Russo-Japanese War
(Sanbechō Shigaku, Ōda City, Shimane Prefecture)

Boxer Rebellion erupted in China under the slogan "Support the Qing, destroy the foreigners," during which Russian troops advanced into Manchuria (northeast China). Japan forged an alliance with Britain, and the Russo-Japanese War broke out in February of 1904. Land battles were fought on the Liaodong Peninsula and a naval battle was fought in the area between present-day Takeshima and Tsushima between the Russian Baltic Fleet and the Imperial Japanese Navy's Combined Fleet commanded by Tōgō Heihachirō. The latter became known as the Battle of Tsushima (Naval Battle of the Sea of Japan).

At the time of the outbreak of the Russo-Japanese War, Nakai Yōzaburō was out hunting sea lions on Lianco Island to test whether it was commercially viable. When he went to Tokyo to submit his request, the war was still ongoing. The government made a cabinet decision that Lianco Island belonged to Shimane Prefecture in January 1905, the name Takeshima was adopted, and the governor of Shimane Prefecture announced to the public what had happened in the form of a notice on February 22 of the same year. The war was ongoing throughout this time.

However, the Battle of Tsushima took place near Takeshima on May 27–28. Neither the dispatch of the Baltic Fleet nor its crossing of the Sea of Japan was anticipated by Japan. Nonetheless, there are researchers who make out a link between the Russo-Japanese War and Takeshima, attempting to justify their theory by saying that Nakai Yōzaburō made his request instigated by the navy or that the navy had positioned a lookout station on the island.

I believe it was incidental that the battle occurred near

Takeshima. Evidence for this is that people from Oki were hunting sea lions on Takeshima at the time of the Battle of Tsushima. Nakawatase Jinsuke, who had taken part in sea lion hunting for more than thirty years from the end of the Meiji period until the early Shōwa period, was fishing near Takeshima at this time. He later recalled how he had seen "the Russian battleships captured right in front of me" in an *Asahi Shimbun* article dated July 7, 1934.

If the government had considered Takeshima a place of strategic importance for the war, then surely, they would not have allowed civilians to fish there. When it comes to the construction of the lookout station, documents related to the navy say that it was constructed in August after the end of the Russo-Japanese War. I am researching the Russo-Japanese War further but have yet to find any source indicating that Takeshima was made part of Shimane Prefecture as part of the war effort.

The most famous connection between the Russo-Japanese War and Takeshima is the newspaper account on the course of the naval battle by Tōgō Heihachirō. It reads, "We forced the enemy ship *Nikolai I* and three other ships to capitulate near the Liancourt Rocks on May 28, while our ships have remained unharmed," but it was soon reported that "Liancourt Rocks is corrected to Takeshima." This was in 1905 and only a few months had gone by since the island's name had changed from Liancourt Island to Takeshima, so that is why the Japanese navy made the mistake, but it is said that this revision made a strong impression on the Japanese people about the existence of Takeshima in the Sea of Japan.

At a monthly poetry gathering of the Ministry of the Imperial Household in June, the theme of "island" was given, upon which a man named Ōkuchi Taiji composed a poem: "The name Takeshima appears like a divine wind dispelling clouds and fog." Another man called Takasaki Shōfū/Seifū recited, "Regularly, sea lions are caught by the fishermen at Takeshima as is, unexpectedly, an occasional whale." Both made explicit references to Takeshima.

17

The Korean Teacher An Yeongjung
in Matsue City in 1905

On February 22, 1905, when it was announced that Take-shima had been officially incorporated into Shimane Prefecture, there was a man named An Yeongjung in Matsue. He was a Korean-language teacher who had come from Korea to Japan, initially working at the Kyoto Prefectural Commercial School. During his time in Kyoto, he opened a small private school called Asahijuku in Kobe. He was a friend of the exiled politician Park Yeong-hyo who was also teaching Korean youth in Japan.

A report dated September 6, 1902, and submitted by the governor of Shimane Prefecture, Kaneo Ryōgen, to Foreign Minister Komura Jutarō says:

On the fifth of this month, the Korean exile An Yeong-jung stayed at the Minamikan in Matsue City in this prefecture. He is a friend of Park Yeong-hyo and others; he has come to Matsue and is traveling the San'in region to sell calligraphy by Park Yeong-hyo and by himself to those interested. This is because he is in need of funds to educate his 24 or 25 students in Kyoto. He has stayed roughly a week and has said that he intends to tour the area around Kizuki-chō, Hikawa District in this prefecture. I would like to report that there is nothing suspicious about his actions.

At this time, the prefectural governor was obligated to report the arrival of any Koreans in the prefecture to the minister of foreign affairs, the minister of home affairs, and the commissioner general of the police. Furthermore, I discuss Park Yeong-hyo, whom An Yeongjung looked up to, in my research report *On Shimizu Jōtarō's Great Map of Korea* as well.

An Yeongjung came to Matsue City once in 1902 and did so again in April the following year as a teacher at Shimane Prefectural Commercial School. According to *Matsue Shōgyō Kōtō Gakkō hyakunenshi* (Matsue Commercial High School 100-Year History), which is a history of the school and its predecessors, "in Meiji 36 [1903], the first principal, Hashimoto Kiichi, was looking for a teacher to teach Korean as he was convinced that Japan and Korea would come to have a close relationship in the future." This leads me to suspect that An Yeongjung had some kind of contact with Hashimoto when he first came to the prefecture in 1902, which opened the door for him to become a Korean-language teacher at this school. Matsue Commercial High School still has An Yeongjung's handwritten résumé.

The people who met him were astonished by his proficiency in Japanese and his résumé shows that he went to a Japanese language school in Korea as well as worked at a government office equivalent to that of the Korean Ministry of Education.

Hashimoto, the one who invited An, had a strong interest in Korea and went on a one-month observation tour of Korea with two student representatives during that year's summer break. His actions indicate that interest in and amicability toward Korea was growing at the school, and it appears that many graduates went to Korea for work. Moreover, Hashimoto later applied to become the principal of the Busan Higher Commercial School in Korea.

An Yeongjung interacted with the people of Matsue City and was especially active as a member of the Chinese poetry association Senshōgin-sha. He was friends with Kowata Kyūemon XIII (pen name Kōu) of the Honjin Kowata family in Shinji-chō, Matsue City. Kōu was a celebrated person of culture who also established a private library in Matsue City. The Kowata family still has a poem written by An Yeongjung himself, which he spontaneously composed about the nature around the Kowata family's vacation home. He dedicated it, "To my elder brother in poetry Kōu, from your Korean younger brother, An Yeongjung."

The Russo-Japanese War broke out in 1904, during An Yeongjung's second year as a teacher at Shimane Prefectural Commercial School. It was a conflict between Japan and

Calligraphy by An Yeongjung (in private possession)

Russia who were both seeking to extend their influence to the Korean Peninsula. At a regular meeting of the Senshōgin-sha that year, the six in attendance wrote linked verse where they took turns to add one line of seven Chinese characters on the theme of victory celebration as Japan won battle after battle in the Russo-Japanese War. While the verses directly represented scenes from the battlefield with lines like "Each of our valiant soldiers has the might of a thousand," when An wrote the fifth line, he made sure that it linked with the others but did not touch on the war. He wrote, "The ambition of the young men is indomitable." The late Iritani Sensuke evaluated it, writing in his book *San'in no kindai kanshi* (Modern Chinese Poetry in San'in), "The line by Kansai [An Yeongjung's pen name] contains the anguish of being among those celebrating victories in a war fought over the control of his homeland."

An left Shimane Prefecture in 1905, and worked as a Korean-language teacher at Nagasaki Higher Commercial School (present-day Nagasaki University) from August that year to March 1907. During this time, he wrote a textbook titled *Kango* (The Korean Language). According to Yamada Hiroto, who currently researches the history of Korean-language education in Japan at Hiroshima University, this textbook was recognized for being easy to understand and was used at many higher commercial schools across the country.

In 1907, when the political exile Park Yeong-hyo returned to Korea following a special pardon by the Korean government, he was accompanied by An. A welcome party for Park was held right after his return, but he could not attend due to ill health so An went on his behalf. A man named Jeong Jaehong snuck in a pistol to the venue with the intention of assassinating Park, but when he was unable to find him, he turned the gun on himself and committed suicide at the party.

In September 1909, An once again came to Japan. He had been invited to work as a Korean-language teacher at Yamaguchi Higher Commercial School (present-day Yamaguchi University), but he was already very ill. He was treated at Akagawa Hospital in Yamaguchi and the University Hospital of Kyoto Prefectural University of Medicine, but never fully recovered. In November 1910, he departed for his homeland to recuperate, but died immediately after arriving in Busan. He was forty-one years old.

18

Nakai Yōzaburō

A brief account of Nakai Yōzaburō's life can be found in *Shōgai kankei tsuzuri* (Documents on Public Relations), an administrative text relating to Takeshima that is held by Shimane Prefecture. Okuhara Hekiun (Fukuichi) also provides a detailed presentation in the recently discovered work *Takeshima keieisha Nakai Yōzaburō-shi risshiden* (Success Story of Nakai Yōzaburō, Manager of Takeshima). According to these sources, Yōzaburō was born in 1864 in Ōaza-Nakagawara, Ogamo Village, Tōhaku District, Tottori Prefecture. His father was called Jinroku and his mother Ura. The family business was a sake brewery. Yōzaburō graduated Shimotanaka Elementary School in 1878, went to Matsue to study, and became a disciple of the Confucian scholar Uchimura Rokō, under whom he studied the Chinese classics. He departed for Tokyo in 1885 to deepen his study of the Chinese classics, but the energy of the metropolis persuaded him to go from academia into business. He concluded his study of the Chinese classics the following year at the age of twenty-three.

According to his résumé, he started engaging in underwater fishing around this time. That is, he was commercially catching sea cucumber, abalone, and so on. I suspect that the diving equipment he used was the kind I saw as a child: a pump onboard a boat that sends air to the diver who is fishing underwater wearing a heavy suit and a round helmet with a large lens. Yōzaburō conducted this business along the shores, including Vladivostok in Russia, Jeolla and Chungcheong Provinces in Korea, Mikuriya in Tottori Prefecture, and Oki and Iwami in Shimane Prefecture.

In 1903, he started planning for sea lion hunting on Lianco Island as part of his fishery business. He felt the need to first gain an understanding of the island, so he headed over to Lianco Island in May of the same year together with Ohara

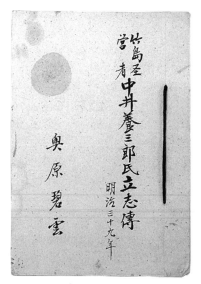

Success Story of Nakai Yōzaburō, Manager of Takeshima (in the possession of Shimane Prefecture Takeshima Reference Room)

Iwazō from the same hometown and Shimatani Gonzō from Oki. In particular, Ohara was to build a cabin on the island and attempt sea lion hunting there two years later. Ohara wrote about this time in a record titled *Takeshima shuttsuryōki* (Record of Hunting at Takeshima).

Yōzaburō was certain that this business was going to be profitable but thought it necessary to clarify the possession of Lianco Island, which is why he wrote *Request for the Territorial Incorporation and Lease of Lianco Island* in 1904. Shimane Prefecture still has a copy of that request. It asks that it be made clear that Lianco Island is Japanese territory, and in the case that it is Korean territory, he requests its lease from the Korean government. It was long unknown why he thought it might be Korean territory. Yet we came to know the reason with the discovery of *Success Story of Nakai Yōzaburō, Manager of Takeshima*. It was because Yōzaburō thought that "the island is Korean territory according to the sea chart."

I believe that sea chart was the *Chōsen zengan* (All the Coasts of Korea), created by the Imperial Japanese Navy in 1896. The sea chart mainly shows the locations of reefs and depths to ensure ship safety and contains no indications of national borders. The characters for *All the Coasts of Korea* are printed in a large font, so the chart obviously depicts the coasts of the Korean Peninsula, but it also includes the Japanese islands Mishima (見島) of Yamaguchi Prefecture and Takashima (高島) of Shimane Prefecture. I believe Yōzaburō was misled by the title *All the Coasts of Korea* and reached the conclusion that Lianco Island might be Korean territory.

Yōzaburō traveled to Tokyo to petition the Ministries of

Home, Foreign, and Agricultural Affairs, and received the support of people like Fujita Kantarō, who worked at the Fisheries Bureau of the Ministry of Agriculture and Commerce. On January 28, 1905, the government made a cabinet decision affirming, "It is clear from the relevant documents that the man named Nakai Yōzaburō has lived and engaged in fishing on the island since Meiji 36 [1903], which means that it has been de facto occupied in accordance with international law, so we see no issue with considering it as belonging to Japan and placing it under the jurisdiction of the governor of the Oki Islands in Shimane Prefecture." The Minister of Home Affairs conveyed this to the governor of Shimane Prefecture. The governor Matsunaga Bukichi

Commemorative photo of the Takeshima Inspection Team immediately after their return (in the possession of Shimane Prefectural Library)

announced it as a prefectural notice on February 22 of the same year.

Now back in Oki, Nakai Yōzaburō applied to the prefecture for permission to hunt sea lions. Besides Yōzaburō, applications were also made by Iguchi Ryūta, Katō Jūzō, and Hashioka Tomojirō, so the governor of Oki, Higashi Bunsuke, advised them to start a joint business and had them establish the Takeshima Fishing and Hunting Limited Partnership Company.

Yōzaburō was representative partner of the Takeshima Fishing and Hunting Limited Partnership Company until 1914 when he passed the position on to his oldest son Nakai Yōichi. Yōichi graduated junior high school under the pre-WWII school system in 1915, after which he personally went out to Takeshima every year and took charge of the company.

Back in Yōzaburō's hometown, there was his nephew Nakai Kinzō, an arts teacher at Tottori Prefectural Kurayoshi Junior High School. He studied under Kuroda Seiki at Tokyo Fine Arts School (present-day Tokyo University of the Arts) and was classmates with Fujita Tsuguharu (also known as Léonard Tsuguharu Foujita) and Okamoto Ippei. In 1909, as a student, Kinzō went to Takeshima looking for painting subjects, producing a record of his experiences there as well as Western-style paintings of Takeshima. The Kurayoshi Municipal Museum in his hometown has more than 20 pieces by him, including his monumental work *Riverbank* (a painting of local women drying squid in Oki), the one hundredth piece of artwork done for his graduation.

19

Uldo Magistrate Shim Heung-taek and the Shimane Prefecture Inspection Team

On February 22, 1905, the governor of Shimane Prefecture Matsunaga Bukichi announced that Takeshima was incorporated into Shimane Prefecture in the form of a notice. In August of that year, he personally traveled to inspect Takeshima together with three prefectural staff members and prefectural police officers. They brought back three Japanese sea lion cubs and tried keeping them in a pond at the prefectural office, but all three soon died and were stuffed instead. The whereabouts of the stuffed sea lions were long unknown, but it was later found that two were at Shimane Prefecture's Izumo Senior High School and Taisha High School. The third one was discovered in March 1999 at Matsue Kita High School. They had all been kept as specimens in their respective science classrooms.

In March 1906, Shimane Prefecture formed an inspection team made up of 45 representatives from all districts, conducted a survey of Takeshima, and sought to gain an overall picture of it. The team leader was Jinzai Yoshitarō, 3rd department chief at Shimane Prefectural Office. Other members included Higashi Bunsuke, Nakai Yōzaburō, Okuhara Hekiun, the principal of the elementary school in Aika Village, Yatsuka District and who later published a detailed record of this survey in *Takeshima oyobi Utsuryōtō* (Takeshima and Ulleungdo).

The ship they traveled on was called the *Okimaru II*. They departed Saigō Port on the evening of March 26, in between several days of bad weather, and reached Takeshima the next morning. Okuhara wrote, "As we approached Takeshima, three orcas violently charged into the ship, countless gulls swooped violently above the water, and thousands of sea lions were congregating and barking on the cliffs." They split up and surveyed the whole island, after which the sea became rough and they traveled to Ulleungdo later that afternoon, which is located 88 km away and where several Japanese had already settled.

Uldo County was established on Ulleungdo in 1900. The Korean royal decree for its establishment stated that the jurisdiction of the county should include all of Ulleungdo as well as Jukdo and Seokdo. The island "Jukdo" here (also written as Bamboo Island, i.e., 竹島/竹嶼) represents present-day Jukdo, also formerly known as Jukseodo, which is an island about 2 km east of Ulleungdo (but not part of present-day Takeshima). When the group from Shimane Prefecture visited there, the county had its district office in Dodong on Ulleungdo, where a county magistrate had been dispatched from the Korean mainland.

Meanwhile, the debate in South Korea has identified this "Seokdo," one of the three islands of Uldo County, as present-day Takeshima. This is the island that is currently at issue between Japan and Korea, and the argument goes that Japan stole the island in 1905 five years after the establishment of

Uldo County. However, there is an article showing the length and breadth of Uldo County in the *Hwangseong Sinmun* (Imperial Capital Newspaper), published in Korea at the time. According to the paper, Uldo County covers an area that is only a short distance from Ulleungdo, making it implausible that it is the same as Takeshima, located some 88 km away. The island described is likely Gwaneumdo Island, which is located near Jukseo.

At the time of the Shimane Prefecture inspection team's visit to Ulleungdo, the Uldo magistrate was a fifty-two-year-old man named Shim Heung-taek. On March 28, more than ten representatives from the Shimane Prefecture inspection team called on the county office and met with Shim. He wore a white robe and a crown, held a long pipe (*kiseru*) used for smoking tobacco, and sat on a floor cushion. Department chief Jinzai explained the reason for the Shimane Prefecture inspection team's visit and presented one of the sea lions they had caught on Takeshima as a gift; in response the magistrate thanked them for coming all the way across the sea as well as for the gift. However, Okuhara wrote in his text that all his answers about the administration of the islands were vague.

After the meeting, the visiting team, Shim Heung-taek, and others at the county office posed for a commemorative group photo. The Shimane Prefecture inspection team departed from Ulleungdo in the evening of that day and headed straight for Saigō Port in Oki. They arrived around four in the afternoon of the next day of March 29.

At the same time, once the inspection team departed, Shim Heung-taek submitted a report dated March 29 (fifth day of the third month in the lunar calendar) to the government of

Gangwon Province, to which Uldo County belonged. It stated, "Dokdo of this county is located more than 100 *ri* away on the open sea, but at the hour of the dragon [7–9 a.m.] on the fourth day of this month, a steamer arrived at Dodong Port on this island and Japanese officials called on our office. And they said that Dokdo is Japanese territory now, so they visited the island to inspect it."

In response to this, Prime Minister Pak Chesoon issued instructions that "there exists no basis on which Dokdo should have become Japanese territory but investigate further and report the status of the island and the actions of the Japanese." Note that both Shim Heung-taek and Pak Chesoon talk about Takeshima using the name Dokdo, which is the name used in Korea today. In Japanese sources, such as

Commemorative photo in front of the Uldo County office (Meiji 39 [1906]) (in the possession of Shimane Prefectural Library)

the *Gunkan Niitaka senji nisshi* (Wartime Journal of the Battleship *Niitaka*) from September 1904, interview data from people who had gone to Takeshima is reported as "the Koreans wrote Dokdo for the Liancourt Rocks, while the Japanese fishermen called it Lianco Island."

Dokdo was not named by a public agency, but I can imagine that Koreans hired by the Japanese to go from Ulleungdo to Takeshima to help with the fishing described the island as "Dokdo" (lit. lonely island) as they saw it as a desolate, far away island. This likely became established and was even used by magistrates like Shim Heung-taek.

Since Shim described Dokdo as "located more than 100 *ri* away on the open sea," we may assume that it was not an island that directly made up the county, like nearby Seokdo, but was only vaguely perceived as belonging to Uldo County.

As mentioned in Chapter 1, in South Korea, they have been publicly naming banks in the seabed around Takeshima after Koreans with great significance to the Takeshima issue. One of those is now named Shim Heung-taek Seamount.

20

The Takeshima Fishing and Hunting
Limited Partnership Company

Last year, there was a report from Okinoshima Town Hall
that residents had found an untended and discarded tombstone at the town's public cemetery with the inscription
"Erected by the Takeshima Fishing and Hunting Limited
Partnership Company." I immediately headed over to con-
firm the find. Inscribed on the front was the name and age
(thirty-four years old) of an individual. On the back, it said
that the Takeshima Fishing and Hunting Limited Partnership
Company was founded in 1907. Tombstones are normally
erected by the deceased's family, so the fact that it was put
up by the company raises several possibilities, such as that
the person was important to the company, that he died in a
company-related accident, or that it was a display of how
well the company was doing.

Following the decision to make Takeshima part of Shimane
Prefecture on February 22, 1905, the prefecture revised its
fishery regulations in April of the same year and made it
possible to apply for sea lion hunting rights on Takeshima.
The Takeshima Fishing and Hunting Limited Partnership
Company was a company that the governor of the Oki Islands

asked permit holders to create in order to conduct the hunting jointly.

Nakai Yōzaburō, who had submitted *Request for the Territorial Incorporation and Lease of Lianco Island* to the government, also warned about "the harm to sea lion colonies from competitive hunting," so he agreed to hunting as a corporate organization. Shimane Prefecture granted permits and licenses to four people with prior sea lion hunting experience on Takeshima: Nakai Yōzaburō, Katō Jūzō, Iguchi Ryūta, and Hashioka Tomojirō. Applications were also submitted by Yodoe Tokuwaka from Uragō Village, Ochi District; Kanō Senkichi from Moriyama Village, Yatsuka District; and

Tombstone erected by the Takeshima Fishing and Hunting Limited Partnership Company (Meiji 40 [1907], Saigō, Okinoshima Town, Oki District)

Shimada Torazō from Akasaki Village, Tōhaku District, Tottori Prefecture, but they were declined.

The company was operating by June of the same year, but their financial statement for fiscal year 1906 states, "In 1906, funds were depleted and credit was minimal due to holdover from the failures of the previous fiscal year," and "The company's finances for this fiscal year did not exceed 800 yen in paid-in capital while the losses of the previous fiscal year were actually as much as 2,500 yen […] Even so, the company has a surplus of 2,200 yen in unpaid capital, so we shall use that to cover the deficit and fund this fiscal year's business."

In January 1907, Saigō Town Hall inquired about the company's finances, and received a response indicative of the less-than-favorable situation of the company in its early years: "3,000 yen in total capital, 1,000 yen in paid-in capital, 1,500 yen in current corporate bonds, no reserves."

In May 1905, the prefecture ordered the Oki Islands Office to accurately survey Takeshima and received a report that it was "23 *chō*, 3 *tan*, 3 *sebu*" (approx. 230,000 m²).* They then made Takeshima into government-owned land and ordered the company to pay a fee. It was 4 yen and 20 sen a year from 1906, which was increased to 4 yen and 70 sen from 1916. This lease of government-owned land and payments of fees was continued in the name of Nakai Yōzaburō, partner of the Takeshima Fishing and Hunting Limited Partnership Company, until 1928. This changed to Yawata Chōshirō from Goka Village between 1929 and 1941.

The company started out with debts, but the sea lion hunting on Takeshima went well. Documents left behind by the company show that they harvested the skins and oil, while the meat and bones were sold west of Osaka as fertilizer. The company-owned ships *Takeshimamaru*, *Chishimamaru*, and *Taiseimaru* were used for this.

Besides sea lion hunting, the company was also allowed to harvest seaweed and to fish for turban shell and abalone around Takeshima, but they were also obligated to sow seeds and plant trees on Takeshima.

Around the time when the Takeshima Fishing and Hunting Limited Partnership Company started increasing revenues in good fashion, poachers started appearing on Takeshima, upon which the company requested Saigō police station to crack down on them. Among them was a man called Naka-watase Jinsuke from Chiran Village, Kawanabe District, Kagoshima Prefecture. He soon became an employee of the company, and eventually became a well-known marksman of sea lions, active on Takeshima for more than 30 years from the Meiji period to the early Shōwa period. The so-called Lianco King, the biggest of the extant stuffed Japanese sea lions, now kept at Tennoji Zoo in Osaka, is said to have been taken down with one bullet from Nakawatase Jinsuke, and the hole can be seen in its head near the ear. The Oki Kyōdo-kan Museum in Goka, Okinoshima-chō also has photo-graphs of sea lion hunting on Takeshima from the Shōwa period.

The Takeshima Fishing and Hunting Limited Partner-ship Company was located in present-day Sashimukō, Nishi-machi, Okinoshima-chō. It was right by the sea, so this is where their ships set out for Takeshima. In June 1907, Hashi-oka Tomojirō and his subordinate Ishida Shinjirō used the company boat *Takeshimamaru* to transport rice and general goods to Takeshima, but were hit by a storm on the way, were unable to reach Takeshima, and ended up in Dodong on Ulleungdo. The record says that on the next day, they forced their way to Takeshima across the rough sea and their ship was badly damaged.

Entering the Taishō period, Nakai Yōzaburō applied to the Hokkaido government office to start a fishery business around Chishima. This was approved and he passed on the rights to the Takeshima Fishing and Hunting Limited Partnership Company to his son Nakai Yōichi. After Hashioka Tomojirō died, his rights were also passed on to his son Tadashige. This was approved after an application was submitted to Orihara Miichirō, the governor of Shimane Prefecture, dated April 30, 1915.

Nakai Yōichi managed the company for a while and crossed over to Takeshima as well but sold his fishing rights to Yawata Chōshirō in 1928 and left Oki.

We can find out quite a lot about sea lion hunting on Takeshima in the Shōwa period from an oral statement left behind by Hashioka Tadashige. Around this time, companies like Kinoshita Circus and Yano Circus were looking for live sea lions to put in a show, so a common method became setting up nets at the entrances to the caves they lived in, chasing them out, and catching them. However, due to overhunting, on one occasion they could only catch 29 animals over 50 days to meet an order of 30, despite Hashioka personally going to the island to lead the effort. Abalone harvesting was conducted in parallel. In charge of that were Korean female divers from Jeju Island, home to many such women. Hashioka paid these women who were risking their lives at the bottom of the sea higher wages than he did the Japanese men hunting sea lions.

The company legally existed until 1926, but the joint endeavor became a mere formality, while independent action by those with fishing rights and the lending of fishing rights for money became common. Hashioka Tadashige transferred his rights to Okumura Heitarō from Kaga, Yatsuka District (present-day Matsue City), who ran a big cannery on Ulleungdo, for a long period of time.

Finally, with the outbreak of the Pacific War in December 1941, fishing around Takeshima ceased entirely.

*According to the Ministry of Foreign Affairs of Japan, Takeshima is 0.2 km² or 200,000 m².

21

Stories from *Friends of Ulleungdo News* (I):
Ulleungdo in 1904 and 1905

Some time ago, Okumura Heiji, a resident of Yonago City, Tottori Prefecture showed me photos of his father and grandfather as well as issues of *Utsuryōtōyū-kaihō* (Friends of Ulleungdo News).

Heiji's grandfather Heitarō built and managed canneries on Ulleungdo and in Masan City (South Gyeongsang Province) on the Korean Peninsula. After his death on Ulleungdo in 1938, management was passed on to Heiji's father Ryō (died in Yonago City in 1989).

The people living on Ulleungdo after World War II formed an association called Friends of Ulleungdo and started publishing a bulletin called *Friends of Ulleungdo News* once a year from 1964. Heiji showed me six years' worth of the bulletin. An issue from a different year had already been found in Nishinoshima, so we now have seven years' worth. Here, I would like to summarize those parts that made a particularly deep impression on me.

First, I noticed that Tamura Seizaburō, who worked at the General Affairs Division of Shimane Prefecture at the time, had published a text titled "Senjin no ashiato, Meiji 37–8-nen no kiroku" (The Footprints of Our Predecessors, Record of 1904–1905) in the bulletin. He wrote an important work organizing the histories of Takeshima and Ulleungdo titled *Shimane-ken Takeshima no shinkenkyū* (New Research on Takeshima, Shimane Prefecture, 1965).

In 1905, the Meiji government decided to make Takeshima part of Shimane Prefecture in January, the governor of Shimane Prefecture announced it to the people in the form of a notice in February, and the navies of Russia and Japan confronted each other near Ulleungdo and Takeshima after the outbreak of the Russo-Japanese War in May.

According to the documents gathered by Tamura, there were 303 Japanese making up 96 households on Ulleungdo as of February 1905. Dividing them by home prefecture, 218 people and 64 households were from Shimane Prefecture and the majority by a wide margin. They were followed by 28 people and 12 households from Tottori Prefecture, and 13 people and 8 households from Saga Prefecture. Yet, considering that the group from Saga consisted of 12 men and only

Friends of Ulleungdo News (in the possession of Shimane Prefecture Takeshima Reference Room)

1 woman, it is likely that it was only one real household and 7 houses with groups of single or migrant worker men. Next came 7 people and 3 households from Wakayama Prefecture, and 7 people and 2 households from Hyōgo Prefecture.

In 1910, Ulleungdo became a Japanese island following the annexation of Korea, and the numbers of people and households doubled. However, we can see that many Japanese had moved to the island even in 1904 and 1905. In total, 181 people comprising 51 households lived in Dodong (called Hamadaura during the Edo period), and some also lived in Namyangdong, Tonggumi, Jukamdong, Taehadong, Sadong, Jeodong, and other places. There were 34 fishermen, 24 sailors, 17 woodcutters, 13 brokers, 13 importers, 9 carpenters, and 3 officials and policemen. There was only one doctor, but no schoolteachers, although there would be many later on.

Even earlier, in June 1902, the Japanese on Ulleungdo had formed a self-governing community with the approval of the Busan Directorate of the Ministry of Foreign Affairs. The bylaws of their Japanese Business Association, in which they decided to jointly contribute funds, suggest that they had hope and determination for rapid progress in a new land. Subsequently, the position of governor of Ulleungdo was created, a leadership position similar to that in the Oki Islands. It would later produce members of the North Gyeongsang Province Assembly on the Korean mainland.

Looking at businesses, Tamura notes, "The fishing businesses are all monopolized by the Japanese, and the Koreans do nothing about fishing. Only the harvesting of wakame is monopolized by the Koreans." He then lists exports of dried squid, dried abalone, and nori seaweed from 1904 and 1905.

He also records that the export of canned abalone started in 1905; this was the start of operations at Okumura Heitarō's cannery. It was no more than 10 boxes for 96 yen in fiscal year 1905, but it was calculated to match market price at four dozen cans per box and 20 sen per can. Total exports were 35,467 yen in 1904 and 71,685 yen in 1905, while total imports of white rice, refined sake, salt, sugar, soy sauce, tobacco, petroleum, cloth, and other consumables from Japan were 16,407 yen in 1904 and 25,480 yen in 1905. Exports were considerably larger and those were two years that really convey the energy of the people uniting in pioneer spirit.

In addition, the material Tamura used for this article matches "Japanese Migrants," which was heading 11 in the chapter on Ulleungdo in Okuhara Hekiun's *Takeshima and Ulleungdo*.

22

Stories from *Friends of Ulleungdo News* (II): Life in the Taishō and Shōwa Periods

The first issue of *Friends of Ulleungdo News* included a register of known residents of Ulleungdo as of October 1964. When compared to the occupations of earlier Japanese residents, we notice new occupations such as those in travel, pharmacists, school faculty, and temple monks in the Taishō and early Shōwa periods.

In 1906, 45 members of an inspection team that included Jinzai Yoshitarō took refuge on Ulleungdo to avoid stormy weather, but there were no inns on the island at the time, so they split up and rested in the homes of three Japanese individuals. After this, the island saw the opening of two inns. Another person in this inspection team was the governor of the Oki Islands, Higashi Bunsuke, but at some point, a similar gubernatorial position in charge of the whole island had been created on Ulleungdo as well. There were also those on the island who had become postmaster, police chief, and principals of the elementary schools in Dodong, Cheonbu, and Taeha.

The recollections of people who lived on Ulleungdo in the early Taishō and Shōwa periods were published in the bulletin. While the editors of the bulletin could not get in contact with any of the successive governors after their return to mainland Japan, the editors did find the following account by a man (Mr. S) who served as governor from 1940 to 1944. The nature of Ulleungdo is described as follows:

The mountains are beautiful and the water pure in Ulleungdo. Winter night gatherings are illuminated under the faint glow of lamps. The snowstorm subsides and the sublime lines of Mount Sankaku [also called Senpō] shine clearly under the bright winter moon. The mountainside is filled with the elegance of rhododendron flowers growing thick around it. For the rest of my days, I shall never forget the deep blue of the calm sea while I was exhausted from swimming at the inlet of Mushige [Jeo-

Ulleungdo Public Elementary School in Dodong, in the eight issue of *Friends of Ulleungdo News* (in the possession of Shimane Prefecture Takeshima Reference Room)

dong]. But what I remember the most vividly in this moment are the white sandalwoods and evergreens growing densely along the precipitous cliffs that made it seem as if the coastline had been sheared clean off. I remember those trees with roots planted deep into the narrow crevices of the rock, displaying a spectrum of colors and shades when shone upon by the sun and moon, exposed to the salty winds coming in from off the surging waves, and always shrouded in a deep green even while enduring the weight of heavy snow. They truly are the symbols of Ulleungdo's cultivation, showing us hope, endurance, a will to live, and gratitude even for poverty.

Another person (Mr. M) grew up on the island from the age of three during the late Meiji period until he and his family had to leave at the end of World War II. He remembers that Mr. S was not only governor but also the police chief. After the war, Mr. M was one of the people, along with one of the Okumura boys, who retold memories of life on Ulleungdo to officials at the Ministry of Foreign Affairs. He left behind many precious recollections:

When I was an elementary school student, we called Ulleungdo "Takeshima," but we knew it said "Matsushima" on sea charts. The Takeshima of today was called "Lianco Island." Regular fishermen didn't go from Ulleungdo to Lianco Island because of fishing rights. Okumura would go diving for abalone every year, and I would harvest wakame from time to time during the Meiji and Shōwa years. You can see Lianco Island clearly from Ulleungdo. You didn't have to go high up on a mountain but could see it clearly from elevated spots. You could see it very clearly on days with bright weather. You could see two triangular shapes. My father was the principal of an elementary school in Ulleungdo and had previously worked as a teacher at an elementary school in Daegu in mainland Korea, and he remembered seeing Ulleungdo from high places [in mainland Korea] such as Uljin and Jukbyeon Bay. He said it looked like a triangle.

It was known that the Okumura family had paid to use the Takeshima fishing rights of Yawata Chōshirō, but if they indeed harvested abalone there every year, it is likely that they were restricted to fishing specific things. Moreover, Ryō Okumura was born in 1911 and of the same generation as Mr. M, so the "Okumura" here likely refers to Ryō.

That you can see Takeshima from Ulleungdo is something we also heard when interviewing an individual from Yatsuka District, Matsue City and another from Okinoshima-chō, Oki District; both were still in good health at the time of this writing. I also recently heard from a Japan Air Self-Defense Force (JASDF) officer that you can see 92 km out from a location elevated 300 m above sea level. Old Korean gazettes also mention that you can see an island with trees and beaches from mainland Korea on clear days, but it was unknown from where you could see Ulleungdo some 140 km away.* However, thanks to Mr. M, we now know that you can see it from elevated places on the mainland like Uljin and Jukbyeon Bay. Mr. M participated in the Ministry of Foreign Affairs interview when he was working as a middle school teacher in Shimane Prefecture in 1953. His name is also on the register of those who returned to Japan and died before 1964.

Many other details were also recollected, such as that Ulleungdo had few paddy fields and had to rely on dry field farming for corn, soybean, hemp, and mulberry and so on, that liners went to Dodong from Busan five times a month and twice a month from Sakai Port, Tottori Prefecture, and that land transportation was inconvenient so they had no carts or bicycles but used small boats to go between the villages to be found in all the inlets.

* I later heard from a reader that sources exist mentioning that Ulleungdo can be seen from Sogongdae and (former) Mangyangjeong.

23

Stories from *Friends of Ulleungdo News* (III):
Interactions with Koreans

The fifth issue of *Friends of Ulleungdo News* was titled *Special Issue on Japanese-Korean Amity*. Relations between Japan and South Korea had been normalized in 1965 and the text of the fifth issue in 1967 is overflowing with memories and feelings expectant of a new bond between the two countries. The Korean consul in Kobe, Lee Weon-dal, who contributed with a text titled "Dedicated to the Friends of Ulleungdo," talked about how he had studied together with Japanese acquaintances from Ulleungdo at a junior high school on the Korean mainland.

Okumura Heiji, who provided me with the volumes of *Friends of Ulleungdo News*, told me that many young people, including Korean students, had been mobilized to his father's cannery in Masan City in mainland Korea as the factory was militarized during World War II.

One current resident of Nishinoshima-chō, told me that the ironworks on Ulleungdo run by her father-in-law and husband had hired two Koreans. When the war ended and they had to return to Japan, the Koreans had entreated them to stay and live together with them on the island, to which they responded that it would cause them trouble if Japanese people remained, and they parted in tears.

The name list in the first issue of the bulletin includes names that are clearly Korean, two individuals from Sadong, and one person from Chusandong are listed as residents of Sakaiminato, Tottori Prefecture. It says that they were born in 1899, 1914, and 1922 respectively, so I believe they came to Japan at the end of the war, hoping to succeed here.

The third issue of the bulletin was published in November 1965. In August of that year, the Friends of Ulleungdo submitted a petition, jointly signed by the president of the association and 77 others, to Prime Minister Satō Eisaku, Minister of Foreign Affairs Shiina Etsusaburō, and others, asking them to clarify Takeshima's (Lianco Island) status as Japanese territory. On June 22, when Japan and South Korea signed the Treaty on Basic Relations between Japan and the Republic of Korea, the issue of who possessed Takeshima was left unresolved. The written resolution states:

> Takeshima is Japanese territory. We are residents of Ulleungdo, North Gyeongsang Province, the place in closest proximity to the contested Takeshima, and have been so since the days of our forebears in the Meiji, Taishō, and Shōwa periods. . . . The island is under the jurisdiction of Shimane Prefecture, and all fishing and harvesting of seaweed is possible only with the approval of Shimane Prefecture, and everyone harvesting abalone, turban shell, red algae, wakame, and the like from Ulleungdo pay fishing fees to license holders in Shimane Prefecture.

One resident of Sakai City, who previously lived on Ulleungdo with their parents, answered a question from a reporter by saying, "Even the Koreans whom we had lived with for many years said that Takeshima was Japanese territory. I want to become a living witness, testifying that Takeshima is Japan's."

In the fifth issue of the bulletin, Mr. S, the former island governor, recalled how they sang "Ulleungdo, although a small island, it is the ideal land of Japanese and Korean harmony, with a deep ancient forest on land and a limitless treasure trove in the sea" to the melody of the Amnok (Yalu) River Tune. In this issue as well as in the sixth issue published in November of 1968, we also find letters and postcards from Koreans speaking about the good old days.

The seventh issue from 1969 contains a section titled "Kankoku yori no tsūshin" (Communication from Korea), reporting that they had received a message from four people who had been together on Ulleungdo before the war.

In the eighth issue from May 1971, we read that the Koreans who remained on Ulleungdo started an organization called the Society for the Prosperity of Ulleung County. There is also a text titled "Recently in Ulleungdo" by Lee Yeong-gwan, the society's chairman. Lee wrote a similar report in the ninth issue from May 1973.

The ninth issue contains a report titled "Utsuryōtō ni ittemairimashita" (I Visited Ulleungdo), which describes the author's return to Ulleungdo after some 35 years. He wrote that Dodong Port was in the middle of being expanded, that the island's population was about 25,000, and that the income per capita was the highest in Korea. The report also

Fifth issue of *Friends of Ulleungdo News* (in the possession of Shimane Prefecture Takeshima Reference Room)

includes many photos, showing that houses had already been built on what had once been a graveyard.

The Friends of Ulleungdo was a group of people who valued the bond they shared as a community, Japanese and Korean alike. The group maintained an interest in the Takeshima issue in the postwar period, but unfortunately the group does not exist anymore. We do not know when it was dissolved or how many issues were published in total.

24

Ulleungdo Is a Treasure Island: A Letter from Father to Son

Okumura Heiji called me and said, "I found a text in the form of a letter that my father Ryō left for me." He then sent me a copy but asked that I burn it after reading it since it contained a lot of personal information. It was written in February 1976, and we can deduce from the date that it was written by Ryō when he was 67 years old to his eldest son Heiji when he was 41 years old. It said he wanted to convey "things I haven't talked to you about in detail," and went on to describe the history of the Okumura family, the posthumous Buddhist names and death anniversaries of ancestors, and memories of Okumura Heitarō and his struggles on Ulleungdo. It also contains hope for their descendants and lessons such as not neglecting Buddhist memorial services. It is a touching letter that can be taken as a kind of will. Heiji has no memory of being directly handed the letter, but it seemed he reflected deeply on his father's quiet love. With Heiji's permission, I took information mainly related to Ulleungdo and Takeshima from this letter and have shared them here.

Ryō was adopted by the Okumura family from a family in present-day Izumo City, Shimane Prefecture at age five. His adoptive father Heitarō married the second daughter of the family, but they had no children, so they adopted Ryō, the eighth child of the family, as their eldest son.

The family moved to Ulleungdo, and he was loved by Heitarō and his mother who was also his older sister, so it seems his childhood was a happy one. He spent his childhood on Ulleungdo, enrolled in the fisheries class at Oki Merchant Marine and Fisheries School, which later became Shimane Prefectural Oki Fisheries High School, and graduated in March 1928. As already noted, Heitarō ran a cannery, and they sent their first shipment in 1905. Business seems to have gone well after this as he also had three factories on Ulleungdo.

Upon graduation, he put to use the specialized knowledge that he had acquired, worked as an assistant to his father,

Left, father Ryō; and *right*, son Heiji (in private possession)

and produced good results. Some years they were the number one producers of canned mackerel in Japan, and they exported to mainland Japan as well as to Southeast Asia. His mother was tough as well, admirably leading the 300 employees on Ulleungdo, so that Heitarō could expand to mainland Korea and build a factory in Jumunjin (Gangneung City), Gangwon Province. Ryō then expanded business to Masan City. It appears that Heitarō often said, "When we went to Ulleungdo, the island had many trees, the fish came all the way up to the shore, and shellfish, especially abalone and turban shell, completely covered the rocks. I really thought of it as a treasure island."

As the business expanded, demand also grew, so they purchased a permit to harvest abalone, turban shell, and the like (excluding only sea lions) on present-day Takeshima for three years from the prominent figure Yawata Chōshirō. This was at a time when they were still crossing over to the islands by sailboat, so boats fishing at Takeshima would often collide with the reefs.

In 1933, Ryō married the eldest daughter of a family conducting extensive business in Gangwon Province, and the two had Heiji and a daughter. Ryō was at the pinnacle of happiness, but then his mother/older sister died in 1934. On March 9, 1938, he lost his wife at the young age of 28 in the morning and his adoptive father Heitarō at the age of 57 in the evening. Both died at Kyushu University Hospital, where they had been taken for care. Ryō documented his grief on losing two family members on the same day in writing that reads with palpable sorrow.

Now the time had finally come for Ryō to take charge of

the Okumura family. He was twenty-nine years old at the time. Ryō dedicates some lines to reminisce about his pride over struggling and working hard to produce results in the two years from 1938. In that year, he personally entered into a contract with Yawata Chōshiro to gain fishing rights for Takeshima, after which he started going to Takeshima via motorboat.

Ryō was interviewed by people from Shimane Prefecture in 1953 and 1954 and spoke extensively about Takeshima. Looking at this newly discovered document, I found that there was a part on the final page that had been crossed out with a pen titled "Memo: On Takeshima." This is unfortunate, as I would have liked to have known his thoughts about Takeshima in 1976.

Ryō remarried, wedding a woman from Matsue in 1940. He writes that he was happy that his son and daughter soon grew fond of their new mother and that his wife loved them. He also wanted to apologize to Heiji for often being away from home and making them feel lonely.

As the Pacific War intensified, the Okumura canneries were militarized, and they started canning not only fish and shellfish, but also beef. He also wrote about the pain of the wartime years and about returning from Korea after the war.

This nine-page letter from father to son is a valuable document for learning about Ulleungdo and Takeshima as well as for making us think about the lives of Japanese people at that point in time.

25

The Pacific War

On September 1, 1939, Germany, which had entered into a military alliance with Italy in May earlier that year, invaded Poland, after which Britain and France, which had a mutual assistance pact with Poland, declared war on Germany. This was the start of World War II. At this time, Japan was waging the Second Sino-Japanese War, and in September 1940, it entered the Tripartite Pact with Germany and Italy. Soon after, Japan invaded French Indochina.

In response to Japan's actions, the United States became increasingly concerned, prohibiting exports of oil and iron to Japan. To overcome this, Japan concluded a neutrality pact with the Soviet Union and dispatched Nomura Kichisaburō, an acquaintance of President Franklin Roosevelt, as the Japanese ambassador to the United States. However, relations with the United States failed to improve, and the Japanese government decided to declare war on the United States, Britain, and the Netherlands at a meeting presided over by the emperor on December 1, 1941. Finally, at 7 a.m. on December 8, a special message was broadcast via radio: "Today, December 8, before dawn, the Imperial Army and Navy entered into a state of war with American and British forces in the western Pacific." By noon, the imperial declaration of war had been sent and the Pacific War had started.

Let us discuss what was happening with Takeshima at this time. Takeshima became part of Shimane Prefecture in 1905, and in the following year Shimane Prefecture started leasing Takeshima as government-owned land for 4 yen and 20 sen a year. Nakai Yōzaburō applied for this and was granted permits in the Meiji and Taishō periods. From 1929 to 1941, applications were made in the name of Yawata Chōshirō, and these were also approved. Yawata was a prominent figure who served as the mayor of Goka Village and had been a member of the prefectural assembly since around 1926. He was also the uncle of Hashioka Tadashige and Ikeda Kōichi who both held Takeshima fishing rights.

There were those who went to Takeshima in June 1940, right before the start of the Pacific War. They were from the Yonago Branch of Mitsui & Co. and went to Takeshima to investigate claims that there was a large amount of mineral phosphate on the island coming from the accumulation of gull guano. They were running low on supplies and thought it could be used as fertilizer.

The late Uchida Ishio from Matsue City testified that he saw three buildings thought to have been built by Nakai Yōzaburō's Takeshima Fishing and Hunting Limited Partnership Company as well as a signpost with the words "Goka Village, Ochi District, Shimane Prefecture" in white paint on the island around this time.* There were those after the war who also invested money into the island's mineral phosphate. We know about these investments from the chapter titled "Takeshima no kōgyōken" (Takeshima Mining Rights) in Tamura Seizaburō's *New Research on Takeshima, Shimane Prefecture*.

At a time when the threat of war was looming, the Ministry of the Navy wanted to use Takeshima as a naval site, and Shimane Prefecture suspended public use on August 17, 1940, and passed it on to the Maizuru Naval District. However, the sea lion hunt was important as it yielded skins and oil, so Yawata Chōshirō made an application to the Ministry of the Navy to use part of Takeshima in February 1941. On November 28 that year, the Ministry of the Navy allowed him to use the island under conditions such as "Use must only be for hunting sea lions, harvesting seaweed and shellfish, and protecting breeding." After this, when Japan surrendered unconditionally in August 1945, jurisdiction over Takeshima's naval site was transferred to the Ministry of Finance in November of the same year.

The cannery run by Okumura Ryō. Shown in the photo are mobilized male students, December 1944. (In private possession)

Meanwhile, regarding fishing at Takeshima, among the verbal accounts recorded by Shimane Prefecture after the war, we find that Hashioka Tadashige caught 16 live sea lions in 1941 and sold them to Kinoshita Circus. Also, in accordance with a contract with Yawata Chōshirō, Okumura Ryō continued harvesting abalone on Takeshima until 1942, but it then appears that he kept going to the island without a contract until 1945.

In the final stages of the war, information that enemy submarines were appearing around Ulleungdo began circulating, so the Okumura family started to think about relocating from Ulleungdo to mainland Korea. Okumura Ryō moved to Masan City on the Korean Peninsula where he had his factory, while the six others, meaning Heiji, Mr. S, the three siblings born from their new mother, as well as the mother, moved to Jumunjin to live with their grandfather,

Mobilized female students working at the cannery, December 1944 (in private possession)

the father of the deceased mother. Returning home to Japan became urgent after the war, so Ryō arrived on a boat in Jumunjin and was finally reunited with his family, but the next day, they were instructed by security forces to gather at the Japanese elementary school with only limited luggage. At the elementary school, they were immediately placed under house arrest. About one month later, they were put on four fish freighters bound for Busan, but the ships were stopped by the US military, and were taken to a nearby port, although they eventually reached Busan.

Ryō remained in Korea in order to take with him some of the assets of the Masan factory, while he had his wife take the five children to Japan. Apparently, this was when the oldest child Heiji was 10 years old, his daughter was 8 years old, and the younger children from the new mother were 4, 2, and 1. Looking back at the letter, Ryō wondered how helpless his wife must have felt jostled by the chaotic crowd, as she boarded the ship with the children.

Ryō himself also soon returned and the family lived in the Asayama area of Izumo City for a while, after which the seven moved to Yonago City. Amid the struggles of the postwar period, the Okumura family had a fresh start.

* "Takeshima ni Shimane no hyōchū" [A Shimane Signpost on Takeshima], *Asahi Shimbun*, June 7, 1977.

26

The Treaty of San Francisco

Following the landing of US forces on Okinawa on April 1, 1945, as well as the nuclear attacks on Hiroshima on August 6 and Nagasaki on August 9, Japan accepted the Potsdam Declaration's demand of unconditional surrender and surrendered on August 15. (The Instrument of Surrender was formally signed on September 2.) Mainland Japan was occupied by the Allies, the General Headquarters (GHQ) was established, and General Douglas MacArthur, Commander-in-Chief, Pacific Command (CINCPAC), arrived in Japan as the first Supreme Commander for the Allied Powers (SCAP). The headquarters, initially located in Yokohama, moved to Hibiya, Tokyo, on September 15. By around 1948, it housed 6,000 staff including 3,850 civilian officials. I was in elementary school back then and remember seeing many Indian soldiers representing the British Commonwealth Occupation Force in Matsue City.

Regarding the territory of Japan, the Cairo Declaration, which was announced in December 1943, had already determined "that Japan shall be stripped of all the islands in the Pacific which she has seized or occupied since the beginning of the First World War in 1914, and that all the territories

Japan has stolen from the Chinese, such as Manchuria, Formosa, and the Pescadores, shall be restored to the Republic of China. Japan will also be expelled from all other territories which she has taken by violence and greed."

Moreover, the Potsdam Declaration from July 1945 states, "The terms of the Cairo Declaration shall be carried out and Japanese sovereignty shall be limited to the islands of Honshu, Hokkaido, Kyushu, Shikoku and such minor islands as we determine."

Since the creation of the GHQ administration, directives were issued by the SCAP and classified according to a Supreme Commander for the Allied Power Index Number (SCAPIN). In particular, I want to bring attention to SCAPIN No. 677, "Governmental and Administrative Separation of Certain Outlying Areas from Japan," from January 1946. It shows areas that were cut off from the control of the Japanese government. They were as follows:

(a) Utsuryo (Ullung) Island, Liancourt Rocks (Take Island) and Quelpart (Saishu or Cheju) Island, (b) the Ryukyu (Nansei) Islands south of 30° North Latitude (including Kuchinoshima Island), the Izu, Nanpo, Bonin (Ogasawara) and Volcano (Kazan or Iwo) Island Groups, and all the other outlying Pacific Islands [including the Daito (Ohigashi or Oagari) Island Group, and Parece Vela (Okino-tori), Marcus (Minami-tori) and Ganges (Nakanotori) Islands], and (c) the Kurile (Chishima) Islands, the Habomai (Hapomaze) Island Group (including Suisho, Yuri, Akiyuri, Shibotsu and Taraku Islands) and Shikotan Island.

Many of these were later returned to Japanese administration, but together with the areas "(a) all Pacific Islands seized or occupied under mandate or otherwise by Japan since the beginning of the world war in 1914, (b) Manchuria, Formosa and the Pescadores, (c) Korea, and (d) Karafuto," described in a separate clause, Takeshima and other islands were considered areas that had to be excluded from Japanese government.

With regard to Takeshima, SCAPIN No. 1033, "Area Authorized for Japanese Fishing and Whaling," which was issued by GHQ in June 1946, states, "Japanese vessels or personnel thereof will not approach closer than twelve (12) miles to Takeshima (37°15' North Latitude, 131°53' East Longitude) nor have any contact with said island," which adds further specificity to their intentions. Takeshima was designated as a bombing practice target for the US military, which continued until June 1953. In the meantime, there were tragedies such as the death of fourteen Koreans, who had gone to the island to harvest wakame, during a bombing exercise in 1948. In 1949, Okumura Ryō saw countless bloodstains on the rocks when he went all the way from Yonago to Takeshima to collect bird droppings for use as fertilizer.

Under the control of the GHQ-led government, Japan enacted the pacifist Constitution of Japan. The following year, it even introduced educational reforms based on the Basic Act on Education and the School Education Act. Alongside Japan's democratization, a rivalry between the United States and the Soviet Union surfaced with the end of World War II and evolved into the Cold War, promoting reconciliation and Japan's return to the international community.

In September 1951, 52 nations who were the victors as the Allied Powers, including the socialist states of the Soviet Union, Poland, and Czechoslovakia, gathered in the United States for the San Francisco Peace Conference. There was an issue of who should represent China. It was between the People's Republic of China, which had consolidated control on the Chinese mainland, and the Republic of China on Taiwan, so neither was invited. India, Burma, and Yugoslavia were also absent.

With the conclusion of the peace treaty came decisions of what to do with Japan's territories. The Occupation ended and there were no more SCAPINs. The question is what happened to Takeshima in the end.

The drafts to the treaty of reconciliation (peace treaty) were first prepared by the US State Department. Until 1949, the State Department drafts stipulated that Takeshima was

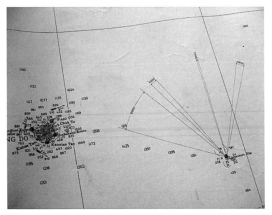

Ulleungdo and Takeshima (Liancourt Rocks) as shown on an American sea chart,1965 (in private possession)

part of Korea. The State Department requested William J. Sebald, US political advisor to MacArthur in Japan, to comment on this November draft, and he advised them to reconsider as Japan's territorial claims on Takeshima were considered both historical and legitimate.

In response to this, Takeshima was added to the areas to remain in Japan's possession, starting with the draft from December 1949. All drafts after August 1950 were written under the guidance of John Foster Dulles, an international lawyer and advisor to the Secretary of State, who oversaw reconciliation with Japan. The drafts were concise and did not specify which islands would be returned, only stipulating the territories that were to be separated from Japan. The Treaty of San Francisco, signed on September 8, 1951, states, "Japan recognizing the independence of Korea, renounces all right, title and claim to Korea, including the islands of Quelpart [Jejudo], Port Hamilton [Geomundo] and Dagelet [Ulleungdo]." We know from the records that South Korea requested that the United States add "Tokto [Dokdo]" to this clause in the final stages of writing the peace treaty. The United States declined this request for revision and stated that Takeshima belongs to Japan's Shimane Prefecture. In this way, it was determined that Takeshima should continue to remain a Japanese territory.

27

The Syngman Rhee Line

The Treaty of San Francisco determined that Takeshima was Japanese territory. In celebration of Takeshima's return to Japanese administration, some of the teachers and students of the fishery class at Tottori Prefectural Sakai High School in Sakaiminato City, went to Takeshima aboard the training ship *Asanagimaru* in November 1951.

The Treaty of San Francisco came into effect in April 1952, but before that, South Korea established the Syngman Rhee Line on January 18. This was a unilateral declaration of maritime sovereignty and Takeshima fell inside that line. It was first thought that the Syngman Rhee Line was designed to bar Japan from the rich fishing waters, particularly to the south of the Korean Peninsula.

The Republic of Korea, created after the war, and Japan had already conducted repeated negotiations over fishing issues, but they were far from reaching an agreement. The Korean side argued that Japanese fishing vessels should not be allowed within certain areas, while the Japanese side argued that this was against the principle of freedom of the high seas. Takeshima was initially not included in the Syngman Rhee Line proposed by the Korean fishery authorities, but it is said that the Korean side added Takeshima for political reasons.

Once the Syngman Rhee Line (called the "peace line" in Korea) was announced, the Japanese government protested that the line was a violation of international waters on January 28 and stated, "It appears that South Korea claims territorial sovereignty over the small island in the Sea of Japan known as Takeshima, but the government of Japan does not acknowledge their pretension or demand." In response to this, on February 12, Korea argued that Korea's territorial claim on Takeshima was supported and confirmed by SCAPIN No. 1033 and the so-called MacArthur Line, which prohibited Japanese fishing vessels from coming less than 12 miles within Takeshima.

Japanese protests and Korean rebuttals continued in this

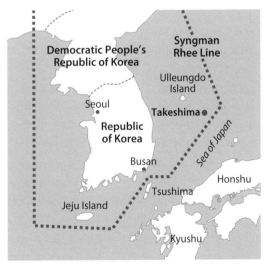

The Syngman Rhee Line (January 1952–June 1965)

way. In May 1953, the research ship *Shimanemaru* of Shimane Fisheries Experiment Station traveled close to Takeshima as part of a survey for the development of the Tsushima Warm Current. They discovered six powered and six unpowered boats with South Korean flags harvesting seaweed and shellfish as well as thirty fishermen. The Japanese government soon protested this, but when the *Shimanemaru* headed out on its second survey, they again saw people on Takeshima. This information was immediately relayed to officials in Shimane Prefecture and Oki. At this time, Ichikawa Tadao, the principal of Oki High School, instructed some fishery class teachers and those with a connection to the fishing industry to investigate the situation on Takeshima by using the school's training ship, the *Ōtorimaru*. Iwataki Katsumi was a fishery class teacher back then and according to him and an article written by an accompanying reporter, there were six Koreans living in tents and collecting seaweed and abalone, waiting for a ship to come pick them up. They had ran out of provisions so they were extremely delighted when the Japanese gave them rice and showed their gratitude by cooking sea lion.

Right after Oki High School's *Ōtorimaru* departed from the island, a joint investigation team from Shimane Prefecture and the Maritime Safety Agency (present-day Japan Coast Guard) arrived on Takeshima. Two officials and three police officers from Shimane Prefecture along with twenty-five officials from the Maritime Safety Agency arrived on Takeshima. In a report submitted to the prefectural governor, the prefectural officials noted the names of the six Koreans and that when questioned, they answered, "We don't know to what country this island belongs, but we come here to harvest wakame every year." The Japanese explained, "This island belongs to Japan so stop coming here," and erected a sign-post marked "Takeshima, Goka Village, Ochi District, Shimane Prefecture." During the Takeshima Day celebrations in Shimane Prefecture on February 22, 2008, images about the history of Takeshima (Dokdo) were uploaded onto a Korean website, including images showing the signpost's removal.

There was one person who saw this removed signpost. It was Date Takeshi, originally from Kaga, Matsue City, and at present a resident of Shimonoseki City. Date was the captain of a Shimonoseki fishing company's trawler and was detained in July 1954 for violating the Syngman Rhee Line near Tsu-shima. He was held for three and a half years. When first taken away by the Busan police, he saw the signpost marked "Take-shima, Goka Village, Ochi District, Shimane Prefecture" ostentatiously lying in a vacant lot. Since he was from Kaga, Shimane Prefecture and familiar with local area names, he distinctly remembers seeing the name on the sign. Date kept a diary throughout his detainment, writing about the difficult days spent not gaining anything with the passing of time.*

During the 13 years from its establishment in 1952 until its termination with the Agreement on Fisheries between Japan and the Republic of Korea of 1965, more than 300 Japanese fishing vessels were unjustly seized for violating the Syngman Rhee Line and nearly 4,000 people were detained. However, many of these vessels were not anywhere near Takeshima when they were seized.

* "Yokuryū Takeshima: Ri Shōban Rain higaisha no shōgen" [Detained Takeshima: Testimonies of Victims of the Syngman Rhee Line], *San'in Chūō Shinpō*, July 15–16, 2007.

28

The *Asanagimaru* and the *Ōtorimaru*

The Treaty of San Francisco was signed in September 1951 and Japan was allowed to rejoin the international community. While Japan was under the GHQ-led government after the war, Takeshima along with places like the Ogasawara Islands and Okinawa were administratively separate from the mainland. Takeshima was used as a practice target for bombing exercises by the US Air Force stationed in Japan, so it was completely off limits. With the signing of the Treaty of San Francisco, administrative control over Takeshima reverted to Japan.

Upon hearing this good news, the fishery class at Tottori Prefectural Sakai High School wanted to check the current state of Takeshima—which would have been partially destroyed after being bombed—and the surrounding area, which was known to be a good area for fishing. On November 13, 1951, a team of six people (four people from the fishery class as well as a reporter and a cameraman from Asahi Shimbunsha) headed for Takeshima aboard the training ship *Asanagimaru*. Yoshioka Hiroshi was a teacher and Yonezawa Akitoshi was an assistant at the school at the time. Yoshioka wrote *Takeshima tokōki* (Record of Crossing over to

Takeshima) immediately after he returned to port, which I borrowed to roughly outline the events that transpired.

At 1 p.m. on November 13, the 16-ton *Asanagimaru* departed Sakai Port and headed out in the direction pointed out by the patrol ship *Suzutsuki*. Ulleungdo to the west of Takeshima came into view at 9:15 a.m. the following morning. They hurriedly adjusted their course with a compass and safely reached Takeshima at 3:30 p.m. They circled Takeshima once in search of a landing point and disembarked on a beach on the eastern islet, Higashijima (東島), also known as Mejima (女島)—the western islet is appropriately named Nishijima (西島), also known as Ojima (男島). The water depth was 570–700 m near where they landed, so even a ship with a big hull would be able to approach it, but there were cliffs all around, making it impossible to moor the ship.

On the eastern islet there was fishing gear that had likely

The crew of the *Asanagimaru* checking the route to Takeshima. Photo taken on November 14, 1951. (In the possession of Shimane Prefecture Takeshima Reference Room)

belonged to Koreans as well as a memorial dedicated to the Koreans who had died in the bombing exercise by the US military. There were caves all around Takeshima, but the eastern islet had an especially large cave that penetrated it vertically and horizontally. They found approximately 100 sea lions in this cave. It was evident that nutritient-rich salt and plankton from the Tsushima Warm Current attracted pilchard, amberjack, mackerel, and squid. Kelp and wakame flourished as well thanks to upwelling from the seabed.

The group departed Takeshima around 5 p.m. on November 14, stopped by Saigō Port at 10:50 a.m. on November 16, and reached Sakai Port at 5 p.m. later that same day. At the very end of his record, Yoshioka writes that there were traces of Koreans continuously coming over to the island in search of marine products, and that if left unchecked, they would eventually claim all rights, prohibit Japanese from going to the island, and proclaim it as their own territory, which is why he hoped that measures would be taken as soon as possible to allow Japanese fishermen to fish there.

However, two months later on January 18, 1952, Rhee Syngman, the first president of the Republic of Korea, made his unilateral declaration of maritime sovereignty and announced that Takeshima and all seas near the Korean Peninsula belonged to South Korea. This was the establishment of the aforementioned Syngman Rhee Line.

Ten days later, the Japanese government formally objected to the government of South Korea. This was one month before the scheduled start of the negotiations to normalize relations between Japan and South Korea, so this caused a major delay to the negotiations.

In 1953, President Rhee Syngman ordered the seizure of Japanese fishing vessels fishing inside the Syngman Rhee Line, and on February 4, the *Daihōmaru I* was seized about 20 nautical miles west of Jeju Island, and the leader of the fishing group was tragically shot and killed. On February 27, the Korean side announced a statement that explicitly claimed possession over Takeshima (Dokdo).

Just as tensions were growing in the waters around Takeshima, the research ship *Shimanemaru*, mentioned previously, conducted a survey of the Tsushima Warm Current on May 28, 1953. They discovered boats with South Korean flags harvesting seaweed and shellfish. In June, the *Shimanemaru* went out for a second survey and again observed people on Takeshima. The Japanese Ministry of Foreign Affairs received a report about this from Shimane Prefecture and sternly objected to the violation of Japanese territorial waters by Korean fishing vessels on June 23.

Not only the people of Shimane Prefecture, but all of Japan felt the tension as they watched events unfold. The training ship *Ōtorimaru*, which belonged to the fishery class of Oki High School, headed out to Takeshima to conduct an on-site investigation, as instructed by the school's principal, Ichikawa Tadao. According to Iwataki Katsumi, who was a fishery class teacher at the time, the *Ōtorimaru* was a 50-ton training ship with seven passengers (according to the article of the *Mainichi Shimbun* reporter who was also there, there were nine), and they reached Takeshima in about eight hours.

There were six Koreans on the island, who were collecting kelp, wakame, and abalone. They had put up tents and were living by the memorial for the Koreans who had died in the bombing incident, which the group from Sakai High School had seen as well. The Ōtorimaru's chief engineer Hara Wahei, who had spent more than twenty years in mainland Korea and was proficient in Korean, addressed them and was told that the ship carrying provisions from Ulleungdo had not come in a while, so they were running out of food. They gave them 6 shō (approx. 10.8 liters) of rice and some tobacco. To show their appreciation, the Koreans caught a sea lion cub and cooked it for the Japanese. The Shimane edition of the *Mainichi Shimbun* from June 27, 1953, had an article with the headline "Mondai no [Takeshima] genchi repo: Mada ita Kankokujin gyofu, ashika no ryōri de kantai" (On-Site Report from Disputed Takeshima: Still-Present Korean Fishermen Entertain with Sea Lion Cuisine).

The Koreans found during the joint investigation by Shimane Prefecture and the Maritime Safety Agency. Photo taken on June 27, 1953, the day after the *Ōtorimaru's* landing. (In the possession of Shimane Prefecture Takeshima Reference Room)

The *Ōtorimaru* returned to Saigō Port in the afternoon of June 26, but something happened before that. A reporter from a certain newspaper company, who had wanted to join the *Ōtorimaru* when it departed but was refused permission, reported the activities of Oki High School to the Shimane Prefecture Board of Education. Since this was right before a secretly planned joint investigation team from Shimane Prefecture and the Maritime Safety Agency was to go to Takeshima, the Board of Education asked Ichikawa Tadao to recall the *Ōtorimaru*. At the time, the departure of training ships in prefectural waters could be decided at the discretion of school principals, so Ichikawa declined the board's request, exercising his authority to conduct a survey of Takeshima as it was within the waters of Shimane Prefecture. The Board of Education reluctantly tried to contact the *Ōtorimaru* by radio, but Iwataki and Hara testified that they were unable to receive it. Ichikawa was urgently summoned to a meeting in Oki and the Board of Education decided to punish him for disobeying their directive.

There are many people in Oki to this day who are discontent with this decision as they had great respect for Ichikawa, a man with a lot of heart and one who acted on strong convictions.

When we conducted interviews about squid fishing around Takeshima with six fishermen from Katae, Mihonoseki-chō, Matsue City on October 24, 2009, one of them, Sasaki Hiroshi, talked about his experience of going to Takeshima on the *Ōtorimaru* and spending three nights there in July 1944 during the Pacific War. Sasaki was a student at Oki Fisheries School before it was integrated into Oki High School and went to the island because he was instructed by the school to survey the phosphorite coming from the accumulation of seabird guano on Takeshima. He told us what he remembered, and more so than the phosphorite survey, the abundance of fish and shellfish that he saw when diving near Takeshima was what left the deepest impression on him.* He has since passed away.

* "Takeshima shūhen de okonawareta ikaryō: Matsue no gyogyōsha ni kikitori" [Squid Fishing around Takeshima: Interviews with Matsue Fishermen], *San'in Chūō Shinpō*, October 25, 2009.

29

Solitary Takeshima:
From the Syngman Rhee Line to
a Provisional Zone

Kuwabara Shisei is a photographer from Tsuwano, Shimane Prefecture. Still active, he is a highly renowned photo-journalist who captured the Minamata disease outbreak in Kyushu and the Vietnam War. In March 1965, he went to South Korea to cover the intensifying student demonstrations opposed to the ratification of the Treaty on Basic Relations between Japan and the Republic of Korea. As Kuwabara finished photographing violent student protests, which included stone-throwing and arrests, he thought about the future of Takeshima. Takeshima's status remained undetermined despite the disappearance of the Syngman Rhee Line. He told a friend that he would like to photograph Takeshima after the abolishment of the Syngman Rhee Line and asked him to make arrangements for a charter flight. As soon as everything was ready, a group of four including the friend and a co-pilot set out for Takeshima.

After the establishment of the Syngman Rhee Line in September 1954, Japan requested that the ROK government submit the question of Takeshima's possession to the International Court of Justice, and otherwise explored options for solving the Takeshima issue. In South Korea, the Rhee

A group from the fishery class at Sakai High School that went to survey Takeshima in November 1951 (in private possession)

Syngman administration fell in April 1960 and was succeeded by the Chang Myon and Park Chung-hee administrations. Kuwabara and his companions picked a route to Takeshima that avoided military radar, and he was able to photograph the dignified solitude of the island rising from the deep-blue sea after no fewer than five nose dives. Shimane Prefecture currently uses a few photos that they have borrowed from Kuwabara.

In December 1965, the Treaty on Basic Relations between Japan and the Republic of Korea, which specified the establishment of diplomatic relations between Japan and South Korea, and the associated Agreement on Fisheries between Japan and the Republic of Korea came into effect, which meant the disappearance of the Syngman Rhee Line. However, the

Takeshima issue was not resolved. In the new Japan-ROK Fisheries Agreement of 1999, which was made during a brief period of warming Japan-ROK relations, vast portions of ocean, including areas near Takeshima, were designated as "provisional zones" that did not belong to either country. In these zones, either country can only manage fishing vessels from their own country. Because of differences in how both countries deal with fishing methods and the preservation of aquaculture resources, this has led to a large number of problems. For example, the Korean method for catching red snow crabs makes it difficult for other vessels to fish in close proximity at the same time. Looking just at Shimane Prefecture, hauls are now only about a quarter of what they were in the past.

In 2005, Shimane Prefecture called for the swift resolution of the fishery and Takeshima issues. Shimane adopted and carried out the "Takeshima Day" ordinance on the 100th anniversary of the cabinet decision that officially incorporated Takeshima into Shimane Prefecture in 1905. Through this, they asked for the interest and cooperation of the people throughout the country.

In July 2008, the Japanese government made it explicit in their *Handbook* that junior high school students should learn about the Takeshima issue in geography class, thereby setting out to expand the young generation's understanding of the Takeshima issue through education.

Takeshima as Japanese Territory

A teacher at an elementary school in Shimane Prefecture published a picture book titled *Aru chiisana chiisana shima no monogatari* (The Story of a Small, Small Island), first in 1995 and then as a revised edition in 2007. The illustrations were also drawn by an artist in Matsue City.

According to the postscript at the end of the book, the teacher had previously worked at a school in Oki and one day, a boy had stared fixedly at him and asked, "Do islands belong to people?" He wrote the picture book based on his memory of that impactful moment. The story is about "a small, small island" where sea lions and seabirds live in peace, but then humans appear. They kill and capture the sea lions, and military aircraft bomb the island for target practice.

The teacher wrote in the book, "The events on the island are based on facts," and that the story accurately depicts what has happened on Takeshima. It seems that the boy's question came at a time when the Takeshima Dispute was frequently discussed in newspapers and on TV. The boy's innocent question touched the hearts of many people through the picture book and became a topic of conversation in

Shimane Prefecture as well. I was moved by this teacher's response to his student's question, which showed a profound love for teaching, and have read the book many times myself, drawn in by the artist's beautiful drawings.

However, lately I feel that I have something that I would like to tell that boy. It's about what a nation is, what territory is, and what the relationship between a country and its people is. A nation appears as something invisible and vague, but it protects the people and its citizens, it protects its territory and domains, and it maintains sovereignty and government. Moreover, each nation maintains relations with other countries by adhering to the United Nations Charter and other aspects of international law and exists in an international community. For example, international law

An illustration from the picture book *The Story of a Small, Small Island*

has rules about how you can acquire territory. The UN Convention on the Law of the Sea also regulates the areas of the sea where each country has rights, such as territorial waters that are within 12 nautical miles (1 nautical mile is 1,852 m) of the coastline of any country facing the sea and the exclusive economic zone that is within 200 nautical miles.

It may be a harsh reality, but in response to the boy's innocent question, although an island belongs to sea lions and seabirds, it also must come under the care of a nation. Our research so far has shown that Takeshima is Japanese territory. Both peaceful human activities and the preservation of the natural environment depend on the establishment of territorial rights.

I imagine the boy has already become an adult by now. I would like to think he has maintained an interest in the ongoing Takeshima Dispute since that day when he asked an innocent question which touched on an aspect of the Takeshima issue.

Just like that boy, I want all junior and senior high school students today to ask questions about Takeshima and take an interest in the issue, which is why I have been bringing up related topics, mainly about the history of Takeshima, through my Sugihara News. With this, my work comes to an end for the time being.

Thank you so much for all the encouragement as well as for your questions and critical feedback. I really feel that I have researched and learned so much. I am more passionate than ever about pursuing a broad engagement of the Takeshima Dispute from here on as well.

Afterword

I wrote this book, but some parts were completed after receiving guidance and corrections from Shimojō Masao, the director of the Web Takeshima Issue Research Institute, as well as from other staff and support personnel. There were also many who read my texts online and informed me about the existence of other sources, leading me to rewrite some parts.

At university I majored in East Asian history and researched the rescue and repatriation of castaways between Japan and Korea in the early-modern period. The words of the late Sumita Nobuyoshi, former governor of Shimane Prefecture, resonated with me when he said, "True friendship between Japan and Korea will be established when we have resolved the Takeshima issue," which is why I have been working on this issue. I think it is superficial to assume that attempting to deal with this issue is something that obstructs friendship with Korea.

When editing this book, I always had in mind junior and senior high school readers, so I did my best to indicate the readings of difficult Chinese characters as well as the readings for Korean names of people and places. I also made a chronology that compares the history of Japan and the San'in region with Korea. Some of my colleagues at the Takeshima Reference Room, Uchida Teruko, Kitamura Kumiko, and Taniguchi Keiko, helped me with the fine proofreading and fact checking, despite their busy schedules. The illustrations on the front and back covers of the Japanese edition were drawn by Fujiwara Fukiko, one of my students when I worked at Shimane Prefectural Matsue Minami High School and who later became vice-principal at an elementary school in the same prefecture. The president of Taniguchi Printing Co. and Harvest Publishing, Taniguchi Hironori, and section chief Fukuda Shūichi helped me with all aspects of the book's publication.

I would also like to thank everyone who contributed to the publication of this English edition. In particular, I would like to express my gratitude to Saitō Kōhei, Ota Hiroko, and Nieda Takami.

This book was born through the warm support of so many people, and it is my hope that it can grab your interest and contribute to a better understanding of the Takeshima issue and its resolution.

Sugihara Takashi

Supplementary Figures

Important illustrations and maps for the study of the Takeshima issue

| 1 | Illustration of Takeshima (Ulleungdo) in the early Edo period |

Present-day Ulleungdo was visited annually by the Ōya and Murakawa families from Yonago as well as Oki fishermen for more than 70 years as they harvested timber, bamboo, sea lions, and abalone. They named the island Takeshima because it was rich in bamboo. The illustration was made in the 1600s and was in the possession of the Murakawa family. Compared to a modern map of Ulleungdo, the shape is slightly off. (In the possession of Yonago Municipal Historical Museum)

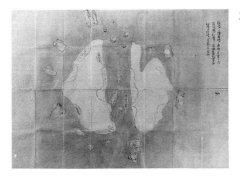

| 2 | Illustration of Matsushima (present-day Takeshima) in the early Edo period |

Matsushima (present-day Takeshima) was discovered en route to Takeshima (present-day Ulleungdo). The Murakawa family frequently went there to hunt sea lions. This illustration, which is said to have been in that family's possession, is almost identical to the latest Korean maps of Takeshima (Dokdo). (In the possession of Yonago Municipal Historical Museum)

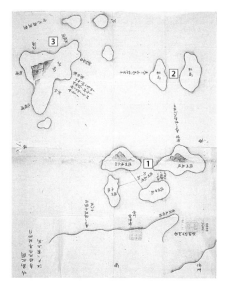

3 | Illustration of Ulleungdo (Takeshima) and Matsushima (present-day Takeshima) submitted to the *bakufu* by the Tottori Domain in 1724

This illustration shows how Yonago townspeople set out from Kumozu in Mihonoseki, passed by Dōzen and Fukuura on Dōgojima in 1) Oki, and crossed over to 2) Matsushima and 3) Ulleungdo (Takeshima). Tottori Domain submitted this illustration at the *bakufu*'s behest during the reign of shogun Tokugawa Yoshimune. (In the possession of Tottori Prefectural Museum)

4 | *Illustration of the Eight Provinces of Korea*

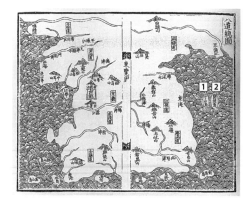

Several versions of the *Illustration of the Eight Provinces of Korea* were made in Korea during the sixteenth and seventeenth centuries. This version shows 1) Usando, a phantom island, to the west of 2) Ulleungdo. Within Korea, there are claims that Usando is Takeshima (Dokdo), but it is believed that the Usando on this illustration was invented using the name of a state called Usan that had existed on Ulleungdo. (*Augmented Survey of the Geography of Korea*, in the possession of Shimane Prefecture Takeshima Reference Room)

5	Map of Ulleungdo from 1711

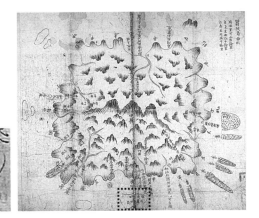

This map shows an island with text indicating that it has 1) a bamboo forest (海長竹田) and is the 2) so-called island Usando (于山島). Since Takeshima (Dokdo) is mostly rocky and much further from Ulleungdo, this Usando cannot be Takeshima. The Usando in this illustration is Jukdo near Ulleungdo. (In the possession of Seoul National University, Kyujanggak Institute for Korean Studies)

6	Nagakubo Sekisui's *Kaisei Nihon yochi rotei zenzu* (Revised Complete Map of Japan with Distances)

This is part of a map of all of Japan by Mito Domain scholar Nagakubo Sekisui. It is thought to be the first map (all previous ones were illustrations) of Japan that uses longitude and latitude lines. It was published in 1779 and reprinted several times. It also shows 1) Takeshima (Ulleungdo) and 2) Matsushima (present-day Takeshima). This particular copy was made in 1846. (In private possession)

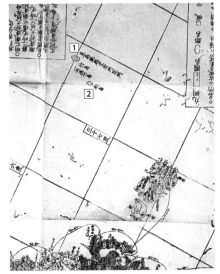

Hayashi Shihei, a scholar active in Sendai Domain, published this map in 1786, although this is a copy made by the Takami family of Izumo. The countries refer to Japan's three neighbors: Korea, the Ryūkyū Kingdom (Okinawa), and Ezo (Hokkaido, Sakhalin, and the Kuril Islands). The map shows 1) Ulleungdo next to the Korean Peninsula, but also mistakenly shows 2) Takeshima, which was the Japanese name for Ulleungdo, on the same map. (In private possession)

8 | European map that shows Argonaut Island and Dagelet Island

In 1787, a French ship surveyed Ulleungdo and named it Dagelet Island. In 1789, a British ship landed on Ulleungdo and named it Argonaut Island. However, the British mischarted the location when surveying Ulleungdo, so it was shown closer to the Korean Peninsula on the map than in reality. European maps started showing Ulleungdo as two separate islands. This is a detail from a map published in Britain in 1835. (In private possession)

9 | Detail of Philipp Franz von Siebold's map of Japan

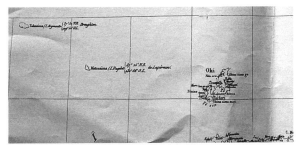

The German physician Philipp Franz von Siebold came to Japan in 1823 to work at the Dutch trading post and brought back home a large volume of materials on Japan. He wrote a book titled *Nippon* and made a map to supplement it in 1840. By this time, he was under the misapprehension that what the Japanese called Takeshima (present-day Ulleungdo) and Matsushima (present-day Takeshima) corresponded to Argonaut Island and Dagelet Island on European maps. In truth, Argonaut Island and Dagelet Island were different names for the same island, Ulleungdo. However, Siebold's map of Japan shows both Takeshima (Argonaut Island) and Matsushima (Dagelet Island). (In private possession)

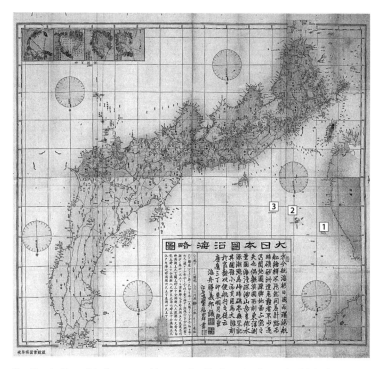

The *Concise Map of the Seas around Japan*, edited by Katsu Kaishū and published in 1867, depicts 1) Takeshima, 2) Matsushima, and 3) Liancourt Island between the Korean Peninsula and Oki. (Reproduction in the possession of Shimane Prefecture Takeshima Reference Room)

11 | *All the Coasts of Korea*, published by
the Imperial Japanese Navy's Waterway Department

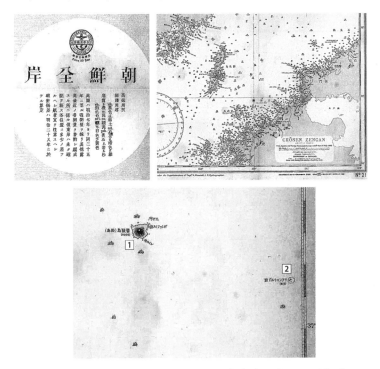

Britain and other countries investigated the location of Takeshima (Argonaut Island), but it was not to be found. The Waterway Department of the Imperial Japanese Navy also conducted surveys of the entire Sea of Japan from the Korean east coast between 1874 and 1892, which resulted in a detailed nautical chart titled *All the Coasts of Korea*. It became clear that Takeshima (Argonaut Island) did not exist, so it only shows 1) Matsushima (Dagelet Island/Ulleungdo) and 2) Liancourt Island. When this Liancourt Island became part of Shimane Prefecture in 1905, it was renamed Takeshima as a way to revive the name that had disappeared, and that brings us to the present. (In the possession of National Institute for Defense Studies)

Chronology

Year	Japan / San'in Region	Korea
194 BC		Wiman becomes king of Gojoseon
108 BC		China (Former Han) advances into northern Korea, establishing Lelang and three commanderies; Gojoseon falls
57 BC		Silla founded in southern Korea
37 BC		Goguryeo (Koguryo), consisting of northern and central parts of Korean Peninsula as well as southern and central parts of Manchuria at its peak, founded
18 BC		Baekje founded in southern Korea
ca. 200	**Shimane**: Burial mounds with four protruding corners become popular	
ca. 300	Gigantic keyhole-shaped mounds (*kofun*) appear in Nara Basin	
313		Goguryeo influence expands significantly, conquering Lelang Commandery
369	Seven-Branched Sword (*Shichishitō*) mentioned in *Nihon shoki* (The Chronicles of Japan) forged with inscription of year and imperial age, held by Isonokami Shrine	
391	War with Baekje and Silla in southern Korea	
ca. 400	**Shimane**: Change to large-scale keyhole-shaped burial mounds	
404	War with Goguryeo in northern Korea ends in defeat	

Year	Japan / **San'in Region**	Korea
413	King of Wa sends envoy to Eastern Jin (China)	
421	King of Wa sends envoy to the Song (China)	
427		Goguryeo moves capital to Pyong-yang
433		Silla and Baekje form alliance
512		Silla conquers Ulleungdo
513	Confucian scholars come to Japan from Baekje	
538	Buddhist statues and scriptures introduced into Japan (thought to be Japan's first encounter with Buddhism)	King Seong of Baekje sends mission to Japan with Buddhist statues and scriptures
593	Prince Shōtoku becomes regent to Empress Suiko	
607	Ono no Imoko dispatched as envoy to the Sui (China)	
630	Inugami no Mitasuki dispatched as first envoy to the Tang (China)	
645	Taika Reforms introduced by Crown Prince Naka no Ōe, Nakatomi no Kamatari, and others	
659	**Shimane**: Izumo Grand Shrine (Kizuki Shrine) built in Izumo by *kuni no miyatsuko* (influential officials during time of Yamato Court)	
660		Silla absorbs Baekje
663	Armies of Japan and Baekje defeated by Tang-Silla forces in Battle of Baekgang (Battle of Hakusukinoe)	
668		Tang (China) conquers Goguryeo
676		Korean Peninsula unified under Silla
684	**Tottori**: Kamiyodo Haiji Temple (ruins of former temple) built in Yodoe around this time	
710	Start of Nara period with capital in Heijō-kyō (present-day Nara)	
712	Compilation of *Kojiki* (Records of Ancient Matters)	

Year	Japan / San'in Region	Korea
716	**Tottori**: Yamanoue no Okura appointed governor of Hōki	
720	Compilation of *Nihon shoki* (The Chronicles of Japan)	
733	**Shimane**: *Izumo no kuni fudoki* written (a record of geography, culture, and folklore of Shimane)	
737	**Yamaguchi**: *Nagato no kuni shōzei chō* written	
741	**Tottori**: Inaba Kokubunji and Hōki Kokubunji temples built	
794	Emperor Kanmu moves capital to Heian-kyō (present-day Kyoto), start of Heian period	
814	**Shimane**: Balhae envoy arrives in Izumo	
863	**Tottori**: People from Silla arrive on Arasaka beach in Inaba	
894	**Tottori**: 105 people from Balhae arrive in Hōki	
918		Wang Geon founds Goryeo (Koryo)
936		Goryeo conquers Silla and unifies Korean Peninsula
996	Fujiwara no Michinaga becomes minister of the left and takes political power **Shimane**: People from Goryeo arrive in Iwami	
1145		Compilation of *Samguk sagi* (History of the Three Kingdoms)
1185	**Yamaguchi**: Minamoto army brings end to Taira clan at Battle of Dan-no-ura in Nagato	
1192	Minamoto no Yoritomo founds first *bakufu* (shogunate), start of Kamakura period	
1221	**Shimane**: Retired Emperor Gotoba banished to Oki	
1237		Production of *Tripitaka Koreana* begins in Goryeo, finishes in 1248 (collection of Buddhist scriptures carved on wooden printing blocks)
1274	Battle of Bun'ei: Mongol-led army made up of Yuan and Goryeo troops invade Japan	Goryeo joins Mongol armies in invasion of Japan (Battle of Bun'ei)

ear	Japan / San'in Region	Korea
36	**Shimane**: Matsuura Takeshirō travels the San'in region	
49	**Shimane**: French whaler *Le Liancourt* names Matsushima (present-day Takeshima) the Liancourt Rocks	
0	**Yamaguchi**: Yoshida Shōin goes to Kyushu for study	
	Commodore Matthew Perry arrives in Uraga from US	
	Perry returns and concludes Convention of Kanagawa **Yamaguchi**: Yoshida Shōin attempts to board USS *Powhatan* in Shimoda (modern-day Shizuoka Prefecture) but caught by *bafuku* officials, taken to Edo, later imprisoned and subsequently put under house arrest in city of Hagi	
	Yevfimiy Putyatin from Russia goes to Shimoda and concludes Treaty of Shimoda between Japan and Russian Empire **Shimane**: British ship captain gives Matsushima (present-day Takeshima) the name "Hornet Rocks"	
	Yamaguchi: Yoshida Shōin founds Shōkasonjuku Academy	
	The Ansei Purge starts when Ii Naosuke becomes chief minister (*tairō*) **Yamaguchi**: Yoshida Shōin arrested again for attempted assassination and revolt	
	Yamaguchi: Yoshida Shōin executed for subversion	
	Naosuke murdered by Mito samurai in Sakuradamon Incident	
		Cartographer Gim Jeong-ho makes *Great Map of the East Land*
	Shimane: Matsue Domain purchases British-made iron-clad battleship and US-made wooden battleship from US; *Yakumomaru 1* and *Yakumomaru 2* respectively	

Year	Japan / San'in Region	Korea
1275	**Yamaguchi**: Outpost established in Nagato to prepare for Mongol attacks	
1285	**Tottori**: Buddhist priest Ippen Shōnin (Zuien) travels around Inaba and Hōki	Compilation of *Samguk yusa* (Memorabilia of the Three Kingdoms)
1332	**Shimane**: Emperor Godaigo banished to Oki	
1333	**Tottori**: Emperor Godaigo escapes Oki to Mount Senjō in Hōki Siege of Kamakura (final battle of Genkō War), fall of Kamakura *bakufu*	
1338	Muromachi (Ashikaga) period begins under shogun Ashikaga Takauji in Kyoto	
1363	**Yamaguchi**: Ōuchi Hiroyo becomes governor of both Suō and Nagato	
1392		Yi Seong-gye conquers Goryeo and founds Joseon
1399	**Yamaguchi**: Ōuchi Yoshihiro takes to arms in Ōei Rebellion and killed	
1408	**Shimane**: Korean goodwill mission deputy envoy Yi Ye drifts to Iwami	
1417		Start of "empty island" policy prohibiting travel to Ulleungdo
1419	Ōei Invasion: Korean army attacks Tsushima	
1420	**Shimane**: Korean king sends letter requesting repatriation of castaways in Yasugi	
1425	**Shimane**: Jang Eulbu drifts to Iwami from Korea, returned by Sufu clan of Iwami	
1426	**Shimane**: Korean king dispatches Yi Ye to Sufu clan with gifts	
1431		Compilation of *Annals of King Taejong*
1443		King Sejong creates hangul (Korean alphabet)
1454		Compilation of *Gazette in the Annals of King Sejong*
1467	Ōnin War starts	
1481		Compilation of *Survey of the Geography of Korea*

Year	Japan / San'in Region	Korea
1524	**Shimane**: Wealthy Hakata merchant Kamiya Jutei develops Iwami Silver Mine	
1542	**Yamaguchi**: Ōuchi Yoshitaka attacks Amago Haruhisa in Izumo	
1549	**Yamaguchi**: Christian missionary Francis Xavier arrives in Yamaguchi	
1561	**Shimane**: Hamada and Mihonoseki included in *Tushupian*, published in China	
1573	Oda Nobunaga banishes Ashikaga Yoshiaki, ending Muromachi *bakufu*	
1582	Honnō-ji Incident: Oda Nobunaga betrayed by general Akechi Mitsuhide, commits seppuku	
1584	Toyotomi Hideyoshi becomes *kanpaku* (chief advisor to the emperor)	
1592	Toyotomi invades Korean Peninsula (Battle of Bunroku)	Japan invades Korean Peninsula (Imjin War)
1597	Toyotomi launches second expedition to Korea	Second Japanese invasion (Chongyu War)
1600	Battle of Sekigahara **Shimane**: Horio Tadauji becomes lord of Izumo and Oki **Yamaguchi**: The Mōri clan forced to relocate to Nagato and Suō	
1603	Tokugawa Ieyasu becomes shogun and founds Edo *bakufu*	
1607	First Korean envoy comes to Japan	
1609		Korea restores agreement with Sō clan of Tsushima Domain and resumes trade
1611	**Shimane**: Matsue Castle completed	
1617	**Tottori**: Ikeda Mitsumasa becomes daimyo of Tottori Domain Ōya Jinkichi of Yonago drifts to Ulleungdo	
1625	**Tottori**: Yonago merchants Ōya Jinkichi and Murakawa Ichibē obtain permission to travel to Ulleungdo	

Year	Japan / San'in Region	Korea
1638	**Shimane**: Matsudaira Naomasa becomes lord of Matsue Domain	
1639	Edo *bakufu* adopts *sakoku* (isolation) policy	
1667	**Shimane**: Matsue Domain retainer Saitō Toyonobu writes *Onshū shichō gōki* (Record of Things Seen and Heard in Oki Province)	
1687	**Shimane**: Administration of Oki transferred from Matsue Domain to governor of Iwami Ginzan	
1693	**Tottori**: Captain of Ōya family boat brings An Yong-bok and Pak Eo-dun to Yonago	
1696	An Yong-bok and ten others return to Japan **Tottori**: Travel to Ulleungdo prohibited	An Yong-bok s Chasando and
1719	**Yamaguchi**: Domain school Meirinkan established	
1726	Tsushima Domain compiles *Takeshima kiji* (Records of Takeshima)	
1728		Compilatio *Sukjong*
1731	**Shimane**: Ido Heizaemon becomes governor of Iwami Ginzan	
1776		Establishm library th and relate dynasty l
1785	Hayashi Shihei publishes *Illustrated Description of Three Countries*	
1804	Russian envoy Nikolai P. Rezanov comes to Nagasaki	
1806	**Shimane**: Inō Tadataka surveys coast from Iwami to Izumo	
1809	British frigate *Phaeton* comes to Nagasaki	
1815	Sugita Genpaku writes *Rangaku kotohajime* (The Beginning of Dutch Studies)	
1823	Philipp Franz von Siebold comes to Nagasaki as physician of Dutch trading post	
1836	**Shimane**: Imazuya Hachiemon arrested and executed for crossing over to Ulleungdo	

Year	Japan / San'in Region	Korea
1863	Chōshū Domain forces fire at American, British, and Dutch ships at Shimonoseki **Yamaguchi**: Takasugi Shinsaku forms militia	
1864	Allied fleet of American, British, Dutch, and French ships bombard Shimonoseki **Shimane**: Start of first Chōshū expedition; San'in domains mobilized to Sekishūguchi	
1866	**Shimane**: Chōshū army takes control of Hamada Domain and Ginzan	
1867	Restoration of imperial rule	
1868	Meiji Restoration, start of Meiji era; outbreak of Boshin War **Shimane**: Riots in Oki **Yamaguchi**: Chōshū-Satsuma army defeats *bakufu* army at Toba and Fushimi	
1871	Abolition of domains and establishment of prefectures; Iwakura Mission departs for US and Europe **Shimane**: Shimane and Hamada Prefectures are created	
1875	Treaty of Saint Petersburg with Russia signed	Ganghwa Island Incident (Japanese battleship *Un'yō* bombarded from Ganghwa Island)
1876	Japan-Korea Treaty of 1876 **Tottori**: Tottori incorporated into Shimane Prefecture	
1881	**Tottori**: Tottori Prefecture reestablished	
1882		Imo Incident: Military confrontation between supporters of Empress Myeongseong (Queen Min) and opponents such as the Daewongun; Japanese legation also attacked
1884		Kapsin Coup: Coup d'état by Park Yeong-hyo, Kim Ok-gyun and other reformists against Korean Sadae-dang administration
1894	First Sino-Japanese War (until 1895)	Donghak Rebellion starts (until 1895)
1895		Eulmi Incident: Assassination of Empress Myeongseong

Year	Japan / San'in Region	Korea
1896	**Tottori**: Sakai Port designated for foreign trade	
1897		Founding of Korean Empire
1904	Russo-Japanese War (until 1905)	
1905	Takeshima incorporated into Shimane Prefecture Korea becomes Japanese protectorate (Itō Hirobumi made first resident-general)	
1909		Itō Hirobumi assassinated by Korean nationalist An Jung-geun in Harbin
1910	Japan annexes Korea (Terauchi Masatake made first governor-general)	Japan-Korea Annexation Treaty signed; Korea annexed by Empire of Japan
1912	Meiji emperor dies; end of Meiji era, start of Taishō period **Shimane**: San'in Railway Line completed (Kyoto-Izumoimaichi)	
1914	Japan joins allied forces in World War I	
1915	Twenty-One Demands made on China	
1918	Rice Riots; Hara Takashi heads the cabinet	
1919	**Yamaguchi**: National Local Specialty Exhibition held	March First Movement
1923	The Great Kantō earthquake	
1925	Public Security Preservation Law and the General Election Law promulgated	
1926	End of Taishō period after death of Taishō emperor, start of Shōwa period	
1929	**Yamaguchi**: Yamaguchi City founded	
1931	Manchurian (Mukden) Incident **Tottori**: Tottori Prefectural Library opened	
1932	May 15 Incident (coup d'état attempt by Imperial Japanese Navy officers)	
1936	February 26 Incident (coup d'état attempt by Imperial Japanese Army officers)	
1937	Start of Second Sino-Japanese War	

Year	Japan/San'in Region	Korea
1940	The Tripartite Pact signed by Japan, Germany, and Italy	
1941	Soviet-Japanese Neutrality Pact concluded; outbreak of Pacific War	
1945	Atomic bombs dropped on Hiroshima and Nagasaki; Japan accepts Potsdam Declaration and capitulates; Allied Occupation of Japan starts	Korean liberation (Japan defeated and Japanese rule of Korea ends)
1946	New Constitution of Japan promulgated	
1948		Republic of Korea (ROK) founded; Democratic People's Republic of Korea (DPRK) founded
1950		Outbreak of Korean War
1951	Japan signs Treaty of San Francisco and US-Japan Security Treaty **Shimane**: Takeshima designated bombing range for US forces by SCAPIN No. 2160	Letter sent from US government to ROK government stating Takeshima is under jurisdiction of Oki Islands branch office, Shimane Prefecture, Japan (Rusk Letter)
1952	Allied Occupation of Japan ends **Shimane**: *Dai Ichi Daihōmaru* Ship Incident	The "peace line" (Syngman Rhee Line) announced, within which Takeshima lies
1953	Amami Islands returned to Japan	Armistice on Korean Peninsula signed
1956	Diplomatic relations restored between Japan and Soviet Union; Japan joins United Nations	
1960	Revision of US-Japan Security Treaty	April Revolution: President Rhee Syngman forced to resign, flees to US
1962		Establishment of Park Chung-hee government
1964	Summer Olympics held in Tokyo	
1965	Treaty on Basic Relations between Japan and the Republic of Korea signed	Treaty on Basic Relations between Japan and the Republic of Korea signed
1967	**Tottori**: Japan–Soviet Union trade and open regular line between Sakai Port and Nakhodka	
1968	Ogasawara Islands returned to Japan	Blue House raid: assassination attempt by North Korean commandos

Year	Japan / San'in Region	Korea
1972	Okinawa returned to Japan; relations between Japan and China normalized	
1973		Kim Dae-jung kidnapped while in Japan and forcefully taken to South Korea
1978	Treaty of Peace and Friendship between Japan and the People's Republic of China concluded	
1979		South Korean president Park Chung-hee assassinated by KCIA director Kim Jae-gyu
1983		KAL 007 Incident
1988		Establishment of Roh Tae-woo government (first democratically elected president of ROK); Summer Olympics held in Seoul
1989	Emperor Hirohito dies marking end of Shōwa period, start of Heisei era	
1992	Bubble economy bursts	
1993		Establishment of Kim Yong-sam government; North Korea Nuclear Crisis (until 1994)
1995	Great Hanshin earthquake	
1997	Asian financial crisis	Asian financial crisis
1998		Establishment of Kim Dae-jung government; start of Sunshine Policy to foster reconciliation with North Korea
2002	Japan co-hosts FIFA World Cup with South Korea	South Korea co-hosts FIFA World Cup with Japan
2005	**Shimane**: Establishment of Takeshima Day	
2007	**Shimane**: Establishment of Takeshima Reference Room	
2008		Establishment of Lee Myung-bak government
2011	Great East Japan earthquake and tsunami; Fukushima nuclear disaster	North Korean dictator Kim Jong-il dies, succeeded by son Kim Jong-un
2012	Japan proposes settling Takeshima Dispute via International Court of Justice	South Korean president Lee Myung-bak makes controversial visit to Takeshima

References

1. One of Kim In-woo's Ships Drifts Ashore in Hamada

Joseon wangjo sillok (Sejong sillok) [Veritable Records of the Joseon Dynasty (Annals of King Sejong), vol. 30]. Twelfth month of Sejong 7.

Joseon wangjo sillok (Taejong sillok) [Veritable Records of the Joseon Dynasty (Annals of King Taejong), vol. 33]. Second month of Taejong 17.

Seki Shūichi. "San'in chihō to Chōsen no kōryū" [Interactions between the San'in Region and Korea]. In *Chūsei Nitchō kaiiki-shi no kenkyū* [Research on Japan-Korea Medieval Maritime History]. Tokyo: Yoshikawa Kōbunkan, 2002.

2. Pioneers to Ulleungdo (Takeshima): Matazai and Ōya Jinkichi

Joseon wangjo sillok (Gwanghaegun ilgi) [Veritable Records of the Joseon Dynasty (Daily Records of Gwanghaegun)]. 1653.

Joseon wangjo sillok (Sukjong sillok) [Veritable Records of the Joseon Dynasty (Annals of King Sukjong)]. 1728.

Kitazawa Masanari. *Takeshima kōshō* [Takeshima Investigation]. 1881.

Nakagawa Akisuke. *Iwami gaiki* [Iwami External Record]. n.d.

"Takeshima tokai yuraiki nukigaki hikae" [Excerpts and Notes on the Origins of Travel to Takeshima]. In *Ōya-ke komonjo* [Ōya Family Documents]. 1868.

"Takeshima tokai kinshi narabi ni tokai enkaku" [Prohibitions on Travel and History of Travel to Takeshima]. In *Tottori-han bunsho 6* [Tottori Domain Documents 6].

Tōfū seisei: Kyūshū Kokuritsu Hakubutsukan kiyō: The Bulletin of Kyushu National Museum, no. 1 (2005).

Yi Maenghyu. *Chungwanji* [Ministry of Rites]. 1744.

3. Ulleungdo and Takeshima

Murakawa-shi kyūki [Ancient Records of the Murakawa Clan].
*in the possession of Historiographical Institute, The University of Tokyo

Ōya-ke komonjo [Ōya Family Documents].
*in the possession of Shimane Prefecture Takeshima Reference Room

Tottori City, ed. *Shinshū Tottorishi-shi dai-2 kan: Kinsei hen* [New Edition History of Tottori City, vol. 2: Early Modern Period]. Tottori: Tottori City, 1988.

4. Ōya Kyūemon and Murakawa Ichibē

Kyōdo shiryō: Murakawa-ke tsuketari Takeshima tokai [Local Sources: The Murakawa Family's Travels to Takeshima].
*in the possession of Yonago Municipal Library

Murakawa-shi kyūki [Ancient Records of the Murakawa Clan].
*in the possession of Historiographical Institute, The University of Tokyo

Okajima Masayoshi, ed. *Inpu nenpyō* [Chronological History of Tottori Domain].
*in the possession of Tottori Prefectural Museum

Ōya-ke komonjo [Ōya Family Documents].

Ōya-shi kyūki [Ancient Records of the Ōya Clan].
*in the possession of Historiographical Institute, The University of Tokyo

Tottori City, ed. *Shinshū Tottorishi-shi dai-2 kan: Kinsei hen* [New Edition History of Tottori City, vol. 2: Early Modern Period]. Tottori: Tottori City, 1988.

Tottori hansei shiryō [Sources of Tottori Domain Administration].
*in the possession of Tottori Prefectural Museum

Tottoriken-shi [History of Tottori Prefecture].
*in the possession of Tottori Prefectural Library

5. Oki and Takeshima

Ikeuchi Satoshi. *Taikun gaikō to "bui"* [Tycoon Diplomacy and "Military Prestige"]. Nagoya: University of Nagoya Press, 2006.

Morisu Kazuo. *Hachiemon to sono jidai: Imazuya Hachiemon no Takeshima ikken to kinsei kaiun, Iwami gaku bukkuretto 3* [Hachiemon and His Time: The Takeshima Incident of Imazuya

Hachiemon and Early-Modern Maritime Transportation, Iwami
Studies Booklet 3]. Hamada: Hamada City Board of Education, 2002.
*Based on the most recent research and writings on the Takeshima map
copied by Watanabe Endayū, it is now held that the correct name is
Imazuya, rather than Aizuya, which used to be the conventional reading.
Saitō Toyonobu. *Inshū shichō gōki* [Record of Things Seen and Heard in
Oki Province].
*According to the research of Ikeuchi Satoshi, 24 copies with partially
different contents have been found, including one in the Shimane
Prefectural Library, one at Shimane University, and one with the
Okinoshima Town Board of Education.
Yada Takamasa. *Chōsei Takeshima ki* [Longevity Takeshima Chronicle].
*in the possession of Shimane Prefectural Library

6. The Genroku Takeshima Incident and the Governor of Iwami Ginzan

Abe-ke monjo [Abe Family Documents].
*in the possession of Iwami Ginzan Silver Mine Museum
Joseon wangjo sillok (Sukjong sillok) [Veritable Records of the Joseon
Dynasty (Annals of King Sukjong), vol. 30]. Tenth month of Sukjong 22.
Katō San'emon. *Kanchō zuihitsu* [Miscellaneous Writings about Things
Seen and Heard].
*in the possession of Ōda Municipal Library
Oki Islands Gazette Editiorial Office, ed. *Okitō-shi* [The Oki Islands
Gazette]. Saigō: Shimane Prefecture Oki Branch Office, 1933.
Oki no kuni utsushi ezu [Copied Illustrations of Oki Province]. In
Muneoka-ke bunsho [Muneka Family Documents].
*in the possession of Muneoka Mitsuaki
Sekishū Ginzan ryō yorozu tekagami [Various Model Cases from Ginzan
of Iwami Province].
*in the possession of Shimane University
Shimane Prefecture, ed. *Shinshū Shimaneken-shi, shiryō hen 2* [New
Edition History of Shimane Prefecture, Historical Materials 2].
Matsue: Shimane Prefecture, 1965.

7. The Korean Goodwill Missions and the Takeshima Issue

Kitajima Manji. *Jinshin Waran to Hideyoshi, Shimazu, Ri Shunshin*
[The Japanese Disturbance in the Imjin Year, Hideyoshi, Shimazu,
and Yi Sun-sin]. Tokyo: Azekura Shobō, 2002.

Matsuda Kō. "Chōsen shinshi to Ōmiji" [The Korean Goodwill Missions and the Ōmi Highway]. *Nissen shiwa* 4 (1976).

Nakao Hiroshi. *Chōsen tsūshinshi to Jinshin Waran: Nitchō kankei-shi ron* [The Korean Goodwill Missions and the Japanese Disturbance in the Imjin Year: History of Japan-Korea Relations]. Tokyo: Akashi Shoten, 2002.

Shin Gisu. *Chōsen tsūshinshi: Hito no ōrai, bunka no kōryū* [The Korean Goodwill Missions: Cultural Exchange and Socialization of People]. Tokyo: Akashi Shoten, 1999.

Song Dae-jung. *Nihon roku* [Record of Japan]. In Shin Gisu and Nakao Hiroshi, eds. *Taikei Chōsen tsūshinshi, zenrin to yūkō no kiroku dai 7-kan* [Survey of Records of Neighborly Relations and Friendship from the Korean Goodwill Missions vol. 7]. Tokyo: Akashi Shoten, 1994.

Sugihara Takashi. "Chōsen tsūshinshi to Un-Seki shohan no futan" [The Korean Goodwill Missions and the Burden on Izumo and Iwami Domains]. *San'in shidan* 17 (1981).

———. "Iwami Ginzan daikan to Chōsen tsūshinshi" [The Governor of Iwami Ginzan and the Korean Goodwill Missions]. *Kyōdo Iwami* 64 (December 2003).

Yonetani Hitoshi, "Kinsei Nitchō kankei ni okeru sensō horyo no sōkan" [The Repatriation of Prisoners of War in Early-Modern Japan-Korea Relations]. *Rekishi hyōron* 595 (November 1999): 28–41.

8. The Japanese Sea Lion and Takeshima

Ōya-ke komonjo [Ōya Family Documents].

Shimane Prefecture Takeshima Issue Research Group. *Takeshima mondai ni kansuru chōsa kenkyū: Chūkan hōkokusho* [Investigation Research on the Takeshima Issue: Interim Report]. Matsue: Shimane Prefecture, 2006.

———. *Takeshima mondai ni kansuru chōsa kenkyū: Saishū hōkokusho* [Investigation Research on the Takeshima Issue: Final Report]. Matsue: Shimane Prefecture, 2007.

Takeshima ikken shorui [Documents on the Takeshima Incident]. 1905–1906.

*in the possession of Shimane Prefecture Public Records Center

9. After the Travel Prohibition

Isotakeshima jiryaku [Abbreviated Matters of Isotakeshima].

*in the possession of University of Tsukuba Library

Kishimoto Satoru. "Bakumatsu kaibō ron to 'kyōkai' ishiki" [The Bakumatsu Naval Defense Debate and Awareness of "Boundaries"]. In *Edo no shisō 9 kūkan no hyōshō* [Edo Thought 9 Symbol of Emptiness], edited by Edo Thought Editorial Committee. Tokyo: Perikan Publishing, 1998.

Life of Matsuura Takeshirō Publication Society, ed. *Matsuura Takeshirō zenshū* [Complete Works of Matsuura Takeshirō]. 1967.

Matsuura Takeshirō Memorial Museum, ed. *Matsuura Takeshirō kinen-kan zuroku* [Illustrated Book of the Matsuura Takeshirō Museum]. Matsusaka: Matsuura Takeshirō Memorial Museum, 1996.

Mori Katsumi. "Kinsei ni okeru Tai-Sen mitsubōeki to Tsushima han" [Tsushima-Korea Smuggling and Tsushima Domain in the Early Modern Period]. *Shien* 45 (1950).

Morisu Kazuo. *Hachiemon to sono jidai: Imazuya Hachiemon no Takeshima ikken to kinsei kaiun, Iwami gaku bukkuretto 3* [Hachiemon and His Time: The Takeshima Incident of Imazuya Hachiemon and Early-Modern Maritime Transportation, Iwami Studies Booklet 3]. Hamada: Hamada City Board of Education, 2002.

Sugihara Takashi. "Hachiemon, Kanamori Kensaku, Matsuura Takeshirō no Takeshima no zu ni tsuite" [About the Illustrations of Takeshima by Hachiemon, Kanamori Kensaku, and Matsuura Takeshirō]. In *Takeshima mondai ni kansuru chōsa kenkyū: Saishū hōkokusho* [Investigation Research on the Takeshima Issue: Final Report] (Matsue: Shimane Prefecture, 2007).

Takeshima kankei bunsho shūsei: Kokuritsu kōbunshokan naikaku bunko shozō "gaimushō kiroku" [Compilation of Takeshima Documents: "Diplomatic Records" Held by the Cabinet Library, National Archives of Japan]. Tokyo: MT Shuppan, 1996.

Yamaguchi Prefecture Board of Education, ed. *Yoshida Shōin zenshū* [The Complete Works of Yoshida Shōin]. Tokyo: Yamato Shobō, 1974.

Yamamoto Mei. *Hokkaidō nazuke oya Matsuura Takeshirō: Ainu minzoku to kōryū shita Isebito no shōgai (Jūrakusen yomuzemi no. 14)* [The Man Who Named Hokkaido Matsuura Takeshirō: The Life of a Man from Ise Who Interacted with the Ainu People (Jūraku Selected Readings no. 14)]. Matsuzaka: Isenokuni, Matsuzaka Jūraku, 2007.

Yadomi Izuo. "Hamada-han Takeshima jiken" [Incidents of Takeshima, Hamada Domain]. *Rekishi dokuhon supesharu* 34, no. 4 (February 1989 special issue).

10. Matsushima Becomes Liancourt Island

Kawakami Kenzō. *Takeshima no rekishi chirigaku teki kenkyū* [A Historical-Geographical Study of Takeshima]. Tokyo: Kokon Shoin, 1966.

Naitō Seichū. *Takeshima (Utsuryōtō) o meguru Nitchō kankei-shi* [History of Japan-Korea Relations over Takeshima (Ulleungdo)]. Tokyo: Taga Shuppan, 2000.

Oki Islands Compilation Official, ed. *Okitō-shi* [The Oki Islands Gazette]. Saigō: Shimane Prefecture Oki Branch Office, 1933.

Shimane Prefecture, ed. *Shinshū Shimaneken-shi* [New Edition History of Shimane Prefecture]. Matsue: Shimane Prefecture, 1965.

Tabohashi Kiyoshi, "Utsuryōtō: Sono hakken to ryōyū" [Ulleungdo: Its Discovery and Possession]. *Seikyū gakusō* 3 (February 1931).

Tamura Seizaburō. *Shimane-ken Takeshima no shinkenkyū: Fukkoku zōho-ban* [New Research on Takeshima, Shimane Prefecture]. Matsue: Shimane Prefecture, 2010.

11. The Tenpō Takeshima Incident and Hachiemon

Kawada Takeo. "Hashimoto Sanpei to Aizuya Hachiemon" [Hashimoto Sanpei and Aizuya Hachiemon]. *Kameyama* 14 (1984).

Morisu Kazuo. *Hachiemon to sono jidai: Imazuya Hachiemon no Takeshima ikken to kinsei kaiun, Iwami gaku bukkuretto 3* [Hachiemon and His Time: The Takeshima Incident of Imazuya Hachiemon and Early-Modern Maritime Transportation, Iwami Studies Booklet 3]. Hamada: Hamada City Board of Education, 2002.

Sugihara Takashi. "Hachiemon, Kanamori Kensaku, Matsuura Takeshirō no Takeshima no zu ni tsuite" [About the Illustrations of Takeshima by Hachiemon, Kanamori Kensaku, and Matsuura Takeshirō]. In *Takeshima mondai ni kansuru chōsa kenkyū: Saishū hōkokusho* [Investigation Research on the Takeshima Issue: Final Report] (Matsue: Shimane Prefecture, 2007).

Yadomi Izuo. "Hamada-han Takeshima jiken" [Incidents of Takeshima, Hamada Domain]. *Rekishi dokuhon supesharu* 15, no. 12 (February 1989 special issue).

12. Matsuura Takeshirō

Takeshima kankei bunsho shūsei: Kokuritsu kōbunshokan naikaku bunko shozō "gaimushō kiroku" [Compilation of Takeshima Documents: "Diplomatic Records" in the Possession of the Cabinet Library, National Archives of Japan)]. Tokyo: MT Shuppan, 1996.

Yoshida Takezō. *Matsuura Takeshirō (Jinbutsu sōsho 142)* [Matsuura Takeshirō (Character Series 142)]. Edited by Nihon Rekishi Gakkai [Japan Historical Society]. Tokyo: Yoshikawa Kōbunkan, 1967.

13. The Japanese Who Crossed over to Ulleungdo in the Early Meiji Period

Kikyō Mutsuto. "Meiji 16-nen Utsuryōtō ikken" [The Meiji 16 Ulleungdo Incident]. *Yamaguchi-ken chihō shi kenkyū* [Yamaguchi Journal of Local History Research] 88 (2002).

Shimojō Masao. *Takeshima wa Nikkan dochira no mono ka* [Does Takeshima Belong to Japan or Korea?]. Tokyo: Bungeishunjū, 2004.

Yi Kyu-won. *Ulleungdo gamchal ilgi* [Ulleungdo Investigation Diary].
   *in the possession of Jeju National Museum

14. The Grand Council of State's Directive in 1877

Chōsen-koku Utsuryōtō e hankin tokō no Nihonjin o hikimodoshi no gi ni tsuki ukagai [Inquiry about the Returning of Japanese Who Illegally Cross over to Ulleungdo, Korea], diplomatic document 3.8.2.4.
   *in the possession of Diplomatic Archives of the Ministry of Foreign Affairs of Japan

Kawakami Kenzō. *Takeshima no rekishi chirigaku teki kenkyū* [Research on the Historical Geography of Takeshima]. Tokyo: Kokon Shoin, 1996.

Naitō Seichū. *Takeshima (Utsuryōtō) o meguru Nitchō kankei-shi* [History of Japan-Korea Relations over Takeshima (Ulleungdo)]. Tokyo: Taga Shuppan, 2000.

Shimane Prefecture Takeshima Issue Research Group, ed. *Takeshima mondai ni kansuru chōsa kenkyū: Chūkan hōkokusho* [Investigation Research on the Takeshima Issue: Interim Report]. Matsue: Shimane Prefecture, 2006.

———. *Takeshima mondai ni kansuru chōsa kenkyū: Saishū hōkokusho* [Investigation Research on the Takeshima Issue: Final Report]. Matsue: Shimane Prefecture, 2007.

Tamura Seizaburō. *Shimane-ken Takeshima no shinkenkyū: Fukkoku zohō-ban* [New Research on Takeshima, Shimane Prefecture: Expanded Reprint Edition]. Matsue: Shimane Prefecuture, 2010.

Tsukamoto Takashi. "Takeshima ryōyūken funsō no shōten (kōen memo)" [The Focus of the Dispute over the Possession of Takeshima (Lecture Notes)]. In *Takeshima mondai ni kansuru chōsa kenkyū, Heisei 19-nendo* [Investigation and Research on the Takeshima Issue for FY2007], edited by Shimane Prefecture (Matsue: Shimane Prefecture, 2008).

15. About *The Chronology of Korea* by Mori Junzaburō

Mori Junzaburō. *Chōsen nenpyō* [The Chronology of Korea]. Tokyo: Ariake Shobō, 1986.

Mori Tomu. "Mori Junzaburō shōden" [A Short Biography of Mori Junzaburō]. *Ōgai* 77 (July 2005).

Museum of Modern Japanese Literature, ed. *Nihon kindai bungaku daijiten, dai-3 kan* [Encyclopedia of Modern Japanese Literature, vol. 3]. Tokyo: Kōdansha, 1977.

Nigaki Torao. "Mori Junzaburō: Ōgai-sensei no mattei" [Mori Junzaburō: Youngest Brother of Master Ōgai]. *Kyōdo Iwami* 24 (1989).

16. The Russo-Japanese War and Takeshima

Denpō Shimbun [The Telegraph], 1903–1906.

Kanpō [Official Gazette], February 10, 1904 and June 5, 1905.

Naitō Seichū. *Takeshima (Utsuryōtō) o meguru Nitchō kankei shi* [History of Japan-Korea Relations over Takeshima (Ulleungdo)]. Tokyo: Taga Shuppan, 2000.
   *in the possession of Shimane Prefecture Public Records Center

"Takeshima" (Meiji 37-nen–41-nen) [Takeshima (1904–1908)].
   *in the possession of Shimane Prefecture Public Records Center

Tamura Seizaburō. *Shimane-ken Takeshima no shinkenkyū: Fukkoku zōho-ban* [New Research on Takeshima, Shimane Prefecture: Expanded Reprint Edition]. Matsue: Shimane Prefecture, 2010.

17. The Korean Teacher An Yeongjung in Matsue City in 1905

Iritani Sensuke and Ōhara Shunji. *San'in no kindai kanshi* [Modern Chinese Poetry in San'in]. N.p.: Society for the Publication of Modern Chinese Poetry in San'in, 2004.

National Institute of Korean History, ed. *Kankoku kindaishi shiryō shūsei: Yō shisatsu Kankokujin kyodō* [Compilation of Sources of Modern Korean History: The Behavior of Koreans under Observation]. 3 vols. Gwacheon: National Institute of Korean History, 2001.

Notsu Seiichirō. *Meiji 36-nen nisshi* [Journal of Meiji 36]. 1903.
   *in private possession

Shimane Prefectural Matsue Commercial High School, ed.
   Matsue Shōgyō Kōtō Gakkō hyakunen-shi [Matsue Commercial High School 100-Year History]. Matsue: Shimane Prefectural Matsue Commercial High School, 2002.

18. Nakai Yōzaburō

Oki Islands Compilation Official, ed. *Okitō-shi* [The Oki Islands Gazette]. Saigō: Shimane Prefecture Oki Branch Office, 1933.

Okuhara Hekiun (Fukuichi). *Takeshima keieisha Nakai Yōzaburō-shi risshiden* [Success Story of Nakai Yōzaburō, Manager of Takeshima]. 1906.
   *in the possession of Shimane Prefecture Takeshima Reference Room

Saigō Town Gazette Compilation Committee, ed. *Saigōchō-shi* [Saigō Town Gazette]. Saigō: Saigō Town, 1975–1976.

Shimane Prefecture Takeshima Issue Research Group, ed. *Takeshima mondai ni kansuru chōsa kenkyū: Saishū hōkokusho* [Investigation Research on the Takeshima Issue: Final Report]. Matsue: Shimane Prefecture, 2007.

Tamura Seizaburō. *Shimane-ken Takeshima no shinkenkyū: Fukkoku zōho-ban* [New Research on Takeshima, Shimane Prefecture: Expanded Reprint Edition]. Matsue: Shimane Prefecture, 2010.

19. Uldo Magistrate Shim Heung-taek and the Shimane Prefecture Inspection Team

Naitō Seichū. *Takeshima (Utsuryōtō) o meguru Nitchō kankei shi* [History of Japan-Korea Relations over Takeshima (Ulleungdo)]. Tokyo: Taga Shuppan, 2000.

Song Byeong-gi. "Nihon no Ryanko-tō (Tokutō) ryōdo hennyu to Utsutō-gunshu Shimu Funteku hōkokusho" [Japan's Territorial Incorporation of Lianco Island [Dokdo] and the Report of Uldo Magistrate Shim Heung-taek]. In *Kankoku kindaishi ronshū* [Essays on Korean Modern History] (Seoul: Jisik Sanup Publications, 1990).

20. The Takeshima Fishing and Hunting Limited Partnership Company

Shōgai kankei tsuzuri (Takeshima kankei tsuzuri) Meiji 28-nen [1895 File on Public Relations (Takeshima)].

    *in the possession of General Affairs Division, General Affairs Bureau, Shimane Prefectural Government

Tamura Seizaburō. *Shimane-ken Takeshima no shinkenkyū: Fukkoku zōho-ban* [New Research on Takeshima, Shimane Prefecture: Expanded Reprint Edition]. Matsue: Shimane Prefecture, 2010.

21. Stories from *Friends of Ulleungdo News* (I): Ulleungdo in 1904 and 1905

Okuhara Hekiun (Fukuichi). *Takeshima oyobi Utsuryōtō fukkoku-ban* [Takeshima and Ulleungdo Reprint Edition]. Matsue: Harvest Publishing, 2005.

    *originally published in 1907 by Hokosha

Tamura Seizaburō. "Senjin no ashiato: Meiji 37–8-nen no kiroku" [The Footprints of Our Predecessors, Record of 1904–1905]. *Utsuryōtōyū-kaihō* 3 (November 1965).

22. Stories from *Friends of Ulleungdo News* (II): Life in the Taishō and Shōwa Periods

Utsuryōtōyū-kaihō [Friends of Ulleungdo News], 1 (October 1964).
Utsuryōtōyū-kaihō [Friends of Ulleungdo News], 3 (November 1965).
Utsuryōtōyū-kaihō [Friends of Ulleungdo News], 5 (November 1967).

23. Stories from *Friends of Ulleungdo News* (III): Interactions with Koreans

Utsuryōtōyū-kaihō [Friends of Ulleungdo News], 1 (October 1964).
Utsuryōtōyū-kaihō [Friends of Ulleungdo News], 3 (November 1965).
Utsuryōtōyū-kaihō [Friends of Ulleungdo News], 5 (November 1967).
Utsuryōtōyū-kaihō [Friends of Ulleungdo News], 6 (November 1968).
Utsuryōtōyū-kaihō [Friends of Ulleungdo News], 8 (May 1971).
Utsuryōtōyū-kaihō [Friends of Ulleungdo News], 9 (May 1973).

24. Ulleungdo Is a Treasure Island: A Letter from Father to Son

    *The content of this section is based on the author's personal correspondence with Okumura Heiji.

25. The Pacific War

Okumura Ryō no kōjutsusho [Oral Statement by Ryō Okumura].
  *in the possession of General Affairs Division, General Affairs Bureau,
  Shimane Prefectural Government

Tamura Seizaburō. *Shimane-ken Takeshima no shinkenkyū: Fukkoku
  zōho-ban* [New Research on Takeshima, Shimane Prefecture: Expanded Reprint Edition]. Matsue: Shimane Prefecture, 2010.

26. The Treaty of San Francisco

Fujiwara Akira. *Taikei Nihon no rekishi 15: Sekai no naka no Nihon*
  [Outline of the History of Japan 15: Japan in the World]. Tokyo:
  Shōgakukan, 1989.

Tamura Seizaburō. *Shimane-ken Takeshima no shinkenkyū: Fukkoku
  zōho-ban* [New Research on Takeshima, Shimane Prefecture:
  Expanded Reprint Edition]. Matsue: Shimane Prefecture, 2010.

Tsukamoto Takashi. "San Furanshisuko heiwa jōyaku ni okeru Takeshima
  no toriatsukai (Heisei 17-nen 9gatsu 27nichi Shimane-ken Takeshima
  Mondai Kenkyūkai 'kenkyū memo')" [The Treatment of Takeshima
  in the Treaty of San Francisco (September 27, 2005 Research Group
  Notes)]. In *Takeshima mondai ni kansuru chōsa kenkyū: Saishū
  hōkokusho* [Investigation Research on the Takeshima Issue: Final
  Report] (Matsue: Shimane Prefecture, 2007).

27. The Syngman Rhee Line

Kawakami Kenzō. *Sengo no kokusai gyogyō seido* [The Postwar International Fishery System]. Tokyo: Japan Fisheries Association, 1972.

Tamura Seizaburō. *Shimane-ken Takeshima no shinkenkyū: Fukkoku
  zōho-ban* [New Research on Takeshima, Shimane Prefecture:
  Expanded Reprint Edition]. Matsue: Shimane Prefecture, 2010.

28. The *Asanagimaru* and the *Ōtorimaru*

Japan-Korea Fishery Council, ed. *Nikkan gyogyō taisaku undō-shi*
  [History of the Japan-Korea Fishery Measure Movement]. Tokyo:
  Japan-Korea Fishery Council, 1968.

Oki Suisan Kōkō sōritsu 70-shūnen kinen-shi [Publication Commemorat-
  ing the 70th Anniversary of the Founding of
  Oki Fisheries High School]. 1983.

Yoshioka Hiroshi. *Takeshima tokō ki* [Record of Crossing over to Takeshima]. 1951.
*in the possession of Shimane Prefecture Takeshima Reference Room

29. Solitary Takeshima: From the Syngman Rhee Line to a Provisional Zone
"Takeshima." *Foto Shimane*, no. 161, special issue (January 2006).
"Tenpūroku: Takeshima no shashin" [Tenpūroku: Photos of Takeshima]. *Chūgoku Shimbun*, March 6, 2008.

30. Takeshima as Japanese Territory
Miyamori Kenji. *Aru chiisana chiisana shima no monogatari* [The Story of a Small, Small Island]. Okuizumo: Pocket Shuppan, 2007.

SUGIHARA TAKASHI

Sugihara was born in Matsue, Shimane Prefecture on May 10, 1938. He majored in East Asian history at Hiroshima University, School of Education. He has previously been a history teacher at Shimane Prefectural Matsue Minami High School, Matsue Kita High School, and Ōda High School. He was also vice-chief of education at the Shimane Prefecture Office of Education and principal of Oki and Matsue Kita High Schools. Sugihara is currently an educator, researcher of regional history, research advisor on the Takeshima issue for Shimane Prefecture, vice-director of the Web Takeshima Issue Research Institute, vice-chairman of the Takeshima Issue Research Group, a member of the Academic Association of Koreanology in Japan, and a member of the Shimane Prefecture History Committee.

〈英文版〉山陰地方の歴史が語る「竹島問題」
The History of Takeshima and Japan:
Historical Accounts and Stories from the San'in Region

2022年2月27日　第1刷発行

著　者　　杉原　隆
英　訳　　公益財団法人日本国際問題研究所
発行所　　一般財団法人出版文化産業振興財団
　　　　　〒101-0051　東京都千代田区神田神保町2-2-30
　　　　　電話　03-5211-7283
　　　　　ホームページ　https://www.jpic.or.jp/

印刷・製本所　大日本印刷株式会社